RUSS KIRKPATRICK

Photo of model for set of the London production of "Not Now, Darling."

NOT NOW, DARLING

A NEW COMEDY

BY RAY COONEY & JOHN CHAPMAN

DRAMATISTS
PLAY SERVICE
INC.

NOT NOW, DARLING was first presented in New York City by James Nederlander and George M. Steinbrenner III, by arrangement with Michael Codron, at the Brooks Atkinson Theatre on October 29, 1970. It was directed by George Abbott; the designer was Lloyd Burlingame; furs were by Monsieur Leon; and the hair stylist was Pierre Hambur. The production supervisor was Ben Janney; and the associate producers were Sheldon B. Guren and Edward Ginsberg. The cast, in order of appearance, was as follows:

MISS WHITTINGTON .... Marilyn Hengst

ARNOLD CROUCH .... Norman Wisdom

MISS TIPDALE .... Joan Bassie

MRS. FRENCHAM .... Jean Cameron

GILBERT BODLEY .... Rex Garner

HARRY McMICHAEL .... Ed Zimmermann

JANIE McMICHAEL .... Roni Dengel

MR. FRENCHAM .... Claude Horton

SUE LAWSON .... Ardyth Kaiser

MAUDE BODLEY .... M'el Dowd

MR. LAWSON .... Curt Dawson

SYNOPSIS OF SCENES

The action of the play takes place in the fourth floor salon of Bodley, Bodley and Crouch, an exclusive London firm of furriers.

ACT ONE

Noon on a day in late September

ACT TWO

Immediately following

3

NOT NOW, DARLING was presented by Michael Codron at the Strand Theatre, London on June 12th 1968, with the following cast:

MISS WHITTINGTON	Ann Sidney
ARNOLD CROUCH	Bernard Cribbins
MISS TIPDALE	Carmel McSharry
MRS. FRENCHAM	Pearl Hackney
GILBERT BODLEY	Donald Sinden
COMMANDER FRENCHAM	Tom Gill
HARRY McMICHAEL	Brian Wilde
JANIE McMICHAEL	Jill Melford
SUE LAWSON	Shirley Stelfox
MAUDE BODLEY	Mary Kenton
MR. LAWSON	David Hargreaves

Directed by Patrick Cargill
Designed by Hutchinson Scott

This play was originally presented at the Richmond Theatre, Richmond on September 18th, 1967, with the following cast:

GILBERT BODLEY	Rex Garner
ARNOLD CROUCH	Ray Cooney
MISS WHITTINGTON	Pamela Merrick
MISS TIPDALE	Stephanie Cole
HARRY McMICHAEL	Ian Gardiner
JANIE McMICHAEL	Lynda Baron
SUE LAWSON	Lisa Peake
MAUDE BODLEY	Mary Allen

4

NOT NOW, DARLING

ACT ONE

The action of the play takes place in the elegant and private 4th floor salon of Bodley, Bodley and Crouch, an exclusive West-end firm of furriers with an esteemed reputation. The hierarchy of the company consists of the three directors, Maude Bodley, her husband Gilbert Bodley and Arnold Crouch.

The decor is opulent and flamboyant and furnished with impeccable taste. The back wall is taken up entirely with French windows through which is a balcony and beyond, the Mayfair skyline. The back section of the set is on a one foot rostrum with stairs leading down L. and R. There are double doors U. L. which lead to the main hall and staircase. A door D. L. conceals an ornate cocktail dispensary. On the inside of the door are glasses, bottles and two tea towels. There is another door D. R. leading to a small storeroom. French windows closed. Doors D. R. and D. L. closed D. Door of double double doors U. L. open. The only pieces of furniture are a splendid round settee D. R. C., a table with two telephones below double doors and a pair of chairs R. and L. of the table.

The time is noon on a sunny day in late September.

As the curtain rises, Arnold Crouch is discovered with two fur-draped models. One of the models is a dummy with legs and the other is Miss Whittington.

The dummy is wearing a £2,000 ocelot. Miss Whittington is wearing a £5,000 Canadian wild mink. Both coats are very modern and beautifully designed. Arnold is putting the finishing touches to the mink brushing it and stepping back to admire his handiwork. He is wearing a long white work coat, and his grey Alpaca jacket is on a chair. After a moment the secretary, Miss Tipdale, enters. She is an efficient, attractive but retiring woman in her early thirties and is wearing a well tailored dress with a zip up the back. *She leaves the door open.*

MISS TIPDALE. Mr. Crouch! Mr. Crouch?
ARNOLD. Ah, good morning, Miss Tipdale.
MISS TIPDALE. Could you spare a moment—? I've got Mrs. Frencham at reception.
ARNOLD. Mrs. Who?
MISS TIPDALE. Mrs. Frencham. *(Indicating.)* For the Ocelot that we've remodelled for her.
ARNOLD. *(Moving to check with the diary on table, picks it up.)* No, no, no, Miss Tipdale. The Ocelot is to be collected at 2.30.
MISS TIPDALE. She is most apologetic, but she's in a hurry.
ARNOLD. I'm sure she is but it hasn't had its final brush yet. And Mr. and Mrs. McMichael are due any minute for the Canadian wild mink.
MISS TIPDALE. Twelve fifteen. *(Referring to mink.)* This is one of your most perfect creations, Mr. Crouch.
ARNOLD. Thank you.
MISS TIPDALE. But the mink is a sale. Mr. Bodley will attend to that. *(During the ensuing dialogue Arnold takes off his white jacket, hands it to Miss Tipdale and puts on his Alpaca jacket.)*
ARNOLD. I sincerely hope so. If and when he arrives. What with he being unpunctual and Mrs. Bodley being on holiday I don't know where I am.
MISS TIPDALE. But what shall I say to Mrs. Frencham?
ARNOLD. You'd better send her in I suppose but this is really Mr. Bodley's pigeon. You know how nervous I get with clients.
MISS TIPDALE. I think you cope splendidly.
ARNOLD. Well— But it is not finished yet and I'll have to explain to her.
MISS TIPDALE. Yes, Mr. Crouch. *(She exits* u. l. *leaving door open.)*
ARNOLD. *(To himself.)* First the ocelot— *(He picks the dummy up between the legs and starts to move it.)* No, *(He puts it down.)* I think perhaps the mink. *(He starts to pick up Miss Whittington in the same way.)*
MISS WHITTINGTON. *(Yells.)* Ahh!
ARNOLD. *(Covered in confusion.)* I'm most terribly sorry, Miss

6

Whittington. I thought you were the er— I'll send for you again when Mr. and Mrs. McMichael arrive.

MISS WHITTINGTON. Thank you, Mr. Crouch. (*Arnold removes the mink from her shoulders and she exits* U. L. *as Mrs. Frencham enters. She is a woman in her late forties and speaks with a frightful Kensington drawl. All her "offs" are "orfs."*)

MRS. FRENCHAM. Am I being very difficult?

ARNOLD. Oh, Mrs. Frencham—! Well as a matter of fact. . . .

MRS. FRENCHAM. I do apologise but my husband and I are in town today shopping, so I thought I'd collect my coat now.

ARNOLD. But, it hasn't had its final brush yet, madam.

MRS. FRENCHAM. Oh, that's all right.

ARNOLD. But I must give it another brush!

MRS. FRENCHAM. Oh very well, I'll come back at lunchtime. I must dash—my husband's driving round the block looking for a parking meter.

ARNOLD. Oh, it is a problem, isn't it?

MRS. FRENCHAM. Yes, next time we'll come on our bicycles! (*Mrs. Frencham exits as Miss Tipdale enters with a catalogue and a note book from* U. L. *door.*)

MISS TIPDALE. Mr. Crouch, are you available for a fitting?

ARNOLD. No, I'm not! This has to be ready at one o'clock. Make a note of that, Miss Tipdale.

MISS TIPDALE. Yes, sir.

ARNOLD. I must get this put away. (*Picking up the dummy.*) Has the 12.15 appointment arrived yet?

MISS TIPDALE. Not yet, no. It's only just gone twelve.

ARNOLD. (*Opens door* D. R. *to storeroom.*) Doesn't anybody ever tidy up in here?

MISS TIPDALE. I'll arrange to have that done later, Mr. Crouch. In the meantime could you check the proofs for the autumn catalogue and see to the fitting downstairs?

ARNOLD. (*Het-up.*) No I couldn't, can't you see I've got my hands full? (*He exits* D. R. *clutching the dummy by the bosom. Miss Tipdale closes the door after him.*)

GILBERT. (*Off, heartily.*) "Morning, all." "Morning, girls." "Morning, Miss Tipdale." Miss Tipdale?! Tippers! Tippers, where are you?

MISS TIPDALE. Here I am, Mr. Bodley. (*From* U. L. *Gilbert Bodley enters. He is a flamboyant extrovert in his late forties with a natural penchant for flowery language and intrigue. He is carrying two bottles of champagne and an umbrella. He is wearing a bowler hat.)*

GILBERT. Good morning, Tippers. How are you?

MISS TIPDALE. *(Doubtfully.)* Well—

GILBERT. Splendid. So am I. What's the time? *(Miss Tipdale pointedly shows him her watch.)* Thank you. *(He hangs his umbrella on her arm and puts his bowler hat on her head.)* What have you got there?

MISS TIPDALE. The autumn catalogue proofs.

GILBERT. Passed. What's next on the agenda?

MISS TIPDALE. The McMichaels at 12.15.

GILBERT. Show them in the moment they arrive. Meanwhile I'll get the champagne on ice. *(Miss Tipdale exits U. L. with umbrella and bowler hat, closing door behind her. Gilbert goes D. L. with champagne and opens cocktail cupboard door disclosing a sumptuous and well-stocked bar. To audience.)* No office should be without one. *(He opens a small "freezer" and puts the champagne in. As he does so.)* That's a lovely load of bubbly. *(Closes bar door, to audience.)* Well, what's a couple of bottles of champagne when you're selling a £5,000 mink? *(He picks the coat up.)* Well, actually, the firm is selling it—but by the strangest coincidence, I'm buying it. Not for myself, you understand. Oh, nothing like that. Oh, no, it's for my girl friend. Now you may well ask what am I, a perfectly happily married man for 20 years doing with a girl friend. Well, it's a pretty soul-searching question— it's a question I've been asking myself for—er—20 years. I'm not exceptional. Statistics prove it. 98 per cent of men are born unfaithful. The other 2 per cent are born liars. But as I was saying, I am buying this coat for Janie McMichael, an exotic beauty of some 28 summers—and 38 bust. Now, there is only one tiny fly in the ointment—Janie's husband. Janie and I feel that he might get a trifle suspicious if she were to arrive home wearing this £5,000 mink. Well, he might. So— I have evolved a scheme of infinite subtlety and some considerable brilliance. *(Takes an envelope from his pocket.)* Here is £4,500 that I have just withdrawn from my private account. When Mr. McMichael arrives here, he will be offered this exquisite coat for £500—cunning, yes? The firm gets its £5,000. Mr. McMichael gets a fantastic bargain for £500—

8

Janie gets her mink and I get—well, that's another story. (*Arnold enters from* D. R. *closing door behind him.*)

ARNOLD. Ah, Mr. Bodley, thank goodness you've arrived. I've been driven out of my mind.

GILBERT. Have we been busy?

ARNOLD. Busy! I've been rushing round like a mad thing!

GILBERT. Good! Keep it up. Have you given that its final brush? (*Gilbert throws coat to Arnold.*)

ARNOLD. (*Catching coat.*) No. And I've asked you before not to be quite so rough with these things. (*Arnold is holding the mink coat. Miss Whittington enters, leaving door open.*)

WHITTINGTON. Mr. Crouch . . . I wonder if . . . Oh, Mr. Bodley, have I time for my coffee break before your 12.15 appointment?

GILBERT. No, you haven't. But would you care for a glass of champagne instead?

ARNOLD. (*Quickly.*) No—no—no, Mr. Bodley, Miss Whittington, up here please. (*He takes her up onto rostrum* C. *and he drapes the coat over her shoulders and gives Gilbert a dirty look as he starts to brush, standing* R. *of her.*)

GILBERT. (*To audience.*) Oh, he's a killjoy, that one. He doesn't belong in either percentage. Look at him. (*Crouch is still fiddling with the coat.*) My partner. We've been together now for 14 years—fourteen agonising, brain-crushing years.

ARNOLD. That's fine. Turn around, please. A little more. Good. Now turn again, Miss Whittington. (*Admires back of coat.*) There's not another one like it in London!

GILBERT. Like what?

ARNOLD. My flared bottom.

GILBERT. (*Laughing.*) Well done, Crouch.

ARNOLD. What?

GILBERT. That was verging on a funny.

ARNOLD. What was?

GILBERT. (*To audience.*) Fourteen years.

ARNOLD. (*Referring to coat.*) Yes, that's lovely. Mr. Bodley, would you care to run your hand over the—

GILBERT. (*He pats her bottom.*) Indeed I would.

ARNOLD. Mr. Bodley! (*Smacks his hand away.*) Thank you, Miss Whittington. I'll send for you again when the McMichaels arrive.

GILBERT. If not sooner. (*Gilbert follows Miss Whittington to door* U. L. *She smiles at him and gently closes it in his face.*)

ARNOLD. Really, Mr. Bodley, how can you when your wife's away?

GILBERT. How can I when she's not?

ARNOLD. Mrs. Bodley would be broken-hearted if she knew as much as I know.

GILBERT. She'd also be pretty stupid. Anyway, what about you and our secretary?

ARNOLD. Miss Tipdale?

GILBERT. (*Sensuously.*) Ambrosine.

ARNOLD. I've never even addressed her as Ambrosine. In all the years she has worked here my conduct towards her has been exemplary.

GILBERT. What! D'you mean you don't fancy her?

ARNOLD. I never said that. Whatever my feelings towards Miss Tipdale might be I would never allow them to jeopardise the efficiency of our organisation. If she and I were to be locked in that storeroom overnight with a crate of champagne she would emerge untarnished. (*Arnold drapes fur on settee, and brushes it.*)

GILBERT. (*To audience.*) The trouble is he means it.

ARNOLD. Mrs. Bodley would be quite horrified if she knew the real reason behind the quick turn-over of models here.

GILBERT. Oh, stop droning on about my wife. She's away on holiday in the South of France, the sun is shining, business is booming. And you're about to conduct your first sale!

ARNOLD. It's all very well— (*Realising.*) I—conduct a sale?

GILBERT. Your finest creation there. (*Indicating mink.*)

ARNOLD. I couldn't possibly when you've instigated the sale with Mr. McMichael.

GILBERT. On the contrary, I've never met Mr. McMichael.

ARNOLD. (*Innocently.*) Oh, I see! Then all your spade-work has been done with Mrs. McMichael?

GILBERT. (*To audience.*) He's getting warm, isn't he?

ARNOLD. I still see no reason why *you* shouldn't complete the transaction.

GILBERT. (*To audience.*) Not as warm as I thought we were. (*He puts his arm around Arnold's shoulder and walks him to* D. R. C. *about below pouffe.*) Arnold! My dear old friend. My dear,

10

dear, dear old friend. Has nothing begun to sink into that brain of yours?

ARNOLD. (*After a pause.*) Mr. Bodley! You haven't formed an association with Mrs. McMichael?

GILBERT. (*To audience.*) My God, he's quick.

ARNOLD. It's appalling, Mr. Bodley.

GILBERT. It's delightful, Mr. Crouch. Oh, I'll never forget that nightclub where I first saw Janie McMichael!

ARNOLD. Nightclub!?

GILBERT. Yes. There she was, dancing away looking as pretty as the day she was born.

ARNOLD. (*Horrified.*) Do you mean to say she's a stripper?

GILBERT. She is a "Striptease Artiste."

ARNOLD. Oh!

GILBERT. A young lady of infinite charm and breeding. Debutante. of the year in 1960. And as you may or may not know that was a vintage year for debs.

ARNOLD. And this is the young lady who is married to Mr. McMichael?

GILBERT. Precisely, and for reasons of my own I wish to lavish Janie with this £5,000 mink, so when Mr. McMichael is offered this unique garment for £500 he'll snap it up.

ARNOLD. £500? We're selling it to him for five *thousand* pounds.

GILBERT. (*Holding out a well-filled envelope.*) Here is £4,500 which I withdrew from my private account this morning. Good luck with the sale.

ARNOLD. It's despicable, Mr. Bodley. Nothing more than payment to Mrs. McMichael for services rendered.

GILBERT. She hasn't rendered anything yet. That's why I'm having to buy the damn thing.

ARNOLD. You mean you haven't yet—er—er—

GILBERT. No, I have not yet "erred." She's a very good girl—but that's all being changed tonight.

ARNOLD. Tonight?

GILBERT. She's told her husband she has a cabaret engagement in Paris and as you know Maude is on holiday.

ARNOLD. Mr. Bodley! You're not taking the young lady round the corner to your penthouse?

GILBERT. Where else? You know I've always been one for my home comforts. Oh, I've organised this one well. Her overnight

11

bag is already there. A profusion of flowers in every room. And the "pièce de résistance," a present laid out on the bed.

ARNOLD. What is it?

GILBERT. A set of frilly lingerie. (*Rubs his hands gleefully.*)

ARNOLD. Damn it, Mr. Bodley, you are—

GILBERT. Lucky is the word you're looking for. (*The internal telephone rings, Gilbert lifts receiver. On phone.*) Hullo . . . Oh, good, they are here. Right. One second. (*He puts the phone down, to Arnold.*) That's Janie and Mr. McMichael. Into battle, Crouch.

ARNOLD. I refuse to participate in such a wicked scheme.

GILBERT. You old woman, you.

ARNOLD. I can't help thinking of your wife all the time.

GILBERT. (*Puzzled.*) Can't you? You must control that!

ARNOLD. You're treating everybody very shabbily.

GILBERT. What are you talking about?

ARNOLD. Well, poor Mr. McMichael mainly. Not only are you trying to steal his wife's affections, you're also getting him to put up £500 towards the expenses.

GILBERT. (*To Arnold.*) I'm doing Mr. McMichael a favour. He'll have a wife who's the envy of the west-end.

ARNOLD. He is still being duped.

GILBERT. Well, for a bloke who's never bought his wife more than a fifty pound sheared raccoon, he's doing very nicely. (*Thrusting money on him.*) You'll cope splendidly, Crouch.

ARNOLD. I don't want anything to do with it. I well remember my father saying "He who touches pitch—"

GILBERT. Just take it. (*As Gilbert tries to force the envelope of money onto Arnold, Miss Tipdale enters.*)

ARNOLD. (*To Gilbert.*) No.

GILBERT. Take it.

ARNOLD. No, I won't.

GILBERT. } (*Together.*) { Take it!
MISS TIPDALE. }   { Excuse me Mr. Bodley—

(*The two men break apart, and Arnold is left holding the money.*)

ARNOLD. (*Flustered.*) Ah, Miss Tipdale—who?—what—why? —when?

MISS TIPDALE. I beg your pardon.

GILBERT. What is it, Tippers? Come, come, come. Stop looking at Mr. Crouch as though he were the last of a dying species. And you, Crouch, stop looking as though you are.

12

MISS TIPDALE. Mr. McMichael is getting impatient.

GILBERT. So am I.

MISS TIPDALE. Shall I show them in?

GILBERT. Yes. (*Gilbert moves to storeroom door.*)

ARNOLD. No! (*To Miss Tipdale.*) Ask them to wait, please.

MISS TIPDALE. I gather Mr. McMichael is in a hurry.

GILBERT. Well, show them in, you silly Tippers.

MISS TIPDALE. Very good, Mr. Bodley. (*She exits* U. L., *closing door.*)

GILBERT. Do your stuff, Crouch. I'll be in the storeroom. (*He throws the fur coat to Arnold.*)

ARNOLD. Something is bound to go wrong. I've never sold a coat in my life!

GILBERT. If you can't sell a £5,000 coat for £500, you must be an absolute idiot!

ARNOLD. I know. Haven't you always said—

GILBERT. Shut up! (*There is a knock at the door. Arnold grabs Gilbert.*)

ARNOLD. (*Frightened.*) You'll have to do it. Knowing what I know I can't possibly face Mr. McMichael.

GILBERT. How do you think I feel, you fool?

ARNOLD. Mr. Bodley! (*Gilbert exits door* R. *Miss Tipdale enters from* U. L.)

MISS TIPDALE. Mr. McMichael's on his way in! Oh Mr. Crouch. Where's Mr. Bodley gone?

ARNOLD. Out of his mind! (*Arnold rushes off* D. R.)

MISS TIPDALE. What about Mr. and Mrs. McMichael? (*Harry and Janie McMichael enter from* U. L. *Harry is a handsome, well-built man in his forties. He is the owner of several gambling casinos. Janie is tall, slender and soigné. She is the epitome of sensual sophistication.*)

HARRY. How much longer are you going to keep us waiting—

MISS TIPDALE. I'm awfully sorry, Sir, but there seems to be some slight . . .

HARRY. Where is everybody?

MISS TIPDALE. Er—I think perhaps they're unwell.

HARRY. What? Mr. Bodley or his partner?

MISS TIPDALE. Well, both seemingly.

JANIE. (*To Miss Tipdale.*) Both of them?

HARRY. There must be SOMEBODY we could see.

MISS TIPDALE. Oh, yes, of course, normally, Mrs. Bodley would be here but she's away on holiday.

JANIE. (*In mock surprise.*) Really? How nice for her.

MISS TIPDALE. Yes, it is actually. She works awfully hard. She won't be back for another fortnight, so I'm afraid . . .

HARRY. Look, just show us this mink coat my wife's been telling me about.

MISS TIPDALE. Well, I'm not quite sure where it—

HARRY. Please go and find it, I have another appointment.

MISS TIPDALE. (*Going to the storeroom door.*) Yes. Do take a seat.

HARRY. Thank you.

MISS TIPDALE. (*Opens door.*) If you could spare a moment, Mr. Crouch or Mr. Bod— (*She is yanked in smartly by Gilbert. As she disappears:*) —ley! (*The door is shut.*)

HARRY. (*Frowning.*) What's going on here?

JANIE. Don't be impatient, darling. There's no rush.

HARRY. I've got to get back to the office and you're catching a plane to Paris.

JANIE. Oh yes, of course, Paris.

HARRY. It's a pity you can't do these one-night stands a bit nearer home.

JANIE. Well, that's show business.

HARRY. If you'd been going later in the week I'd have come with you.

JANIE. Oh, Harry, what a shame.

HARRY. Yes. The syndicate is opening another casino over there. (*Mr. Frencham enters from* U. L., *leaving door open.*)

MR. FRENCHAM. Oh, hello— Is this Bodley, Bodley and . . . ?

HARRY. Yes, it is.

MR. FRENCHAM. Good. Can't stay. Now look, if you see the wife tell her I'm double parked and to wait here while I drop anchor round the corner. Blasted woman's gone off with the six-pences. (*Miss Tipdale re-enters from door* D. R., *pushed in by Gilbert. He shuts door.*) How do you do— Mr. Frencham—can't stay. (*Mr. Frencham exits* U. L., *leaving door open.*)

MISS TIPDALE. Won't be long now, Mr. McMichael.

HARRY. Who is going to show me this mink?

MISS TIPDALE. There seems to be some slight difference of opinion.

14

HARRY. Well, will you tell them to get it sorted out? (*The door* D. R. *opens and Gilbert pushes Arnold out with the mink coat [lining outwards]. Without seeing the others he tries to get back in but Bodley has locked the door. Arnold rattles it.*)

MISS TIPDALE. Mr. Crouch!—

ARNOLD. (*Whipping round.*) It's locked! (*He rattles it again and then realises that he is not alone. Covering up.*) Yes. That's locked. That's definitely locked. We have to be very careful, you know. Make a note of that, Miss Tipdale. "The door is definitely locked at 12.20."

HARRY. (*Pointedly.*) I had an appointment for 12.15. I'm not usually kept waiting.

ARNOLD. I'm terribly sorry. It's been one of those days. Would you like to come back tomorrow and you won't be kept waiting at all?

MISS TIPDALE. (*Nervously.*) Er—Mr. and Mrs. McMichael want to see the coat.

HARRY. Are you sure Mr. Bodley isn't available?

ARNOLD. No, I'm afraid not. I wish he were, but he just doesn't feel up to it.

JANIE. (*Huskily.*) How very disappointing. (*She gives Arnold a knowing wink. He nearly dies.*) I found your Mr. Bodley most charming.

ARNOLD. I'm sure.

JANIE. And very eager to interest me in something.

ARNOLD. I'm sure.

HARRY. (*Innocently.*) Oh, so you're not the man who's been dealing with my wife.

ARNOLD. No!!

HARRY. I am not deaf, Mr.—er—

ARNOLD. Crouch. I'm Crouch. Arnold Crouch. Make a note of that, Miss Tipdale, I'm definitely Arnold Crouch. Arnold with an R—and Crouch with a C,-R,-O,-U, and finishes off with an ouch.

MISS TIPDALE. Is anything the matter, Mr. Crouch?

ARNOLD. (*Shakes head.*) No.

JANIE. Well, I'm sorry Mr. Bodley is not here. But I'm sure Mr. Crouch will be equally helpful. (*Winks again.*)

ARNOLD. (*Flustered.*) Well, I do know that Mr. Bodley would much rather have handled you himself— (*Stops, realising what he's said*.) When I say handled I— (*Mrs. Frencham enters* U. L., *leaving door open. She comes down* C. *steps and to* L. *of Miss Tipdale*.)

MRS. FRENCHAM. (*As she enters*.) George! George! (*Sees Harry and Janie*.) Oh, do forgive me. Have you seen my husband, Miss Tipdale?

MISS TIPDALE. Well, not actually to talk to.

MRS. FRENCHAM. Oh, dear. Your doorman has found us a parking meter, and now I've lost my husband!

JANIE. He was here just a moment ago.

MRS. FRENCHAM. Missed him again! He must have gone down in the elevator. I'm using the stairs these days. Good for the tum-tum. (*She exits* U. L., *leaving door open*.)

HARRY. If it wouldn't be too much to ask, Mr.—er—

ARNOLD. —er—

MISS TIPDALE. Crouch.

ARNOLD. Crouch.

HARRY. Yes, Crouch.

ARNOLD. Arnold Crouch.

HARRY. Yes. Just show us the mink.

ARNOLD. Ah, yes. The mink. Now where is it?

HARRY. I don't know where it is.

MISS TIPDALE. (*Pointing to coat over Arnold's arm*.) Isn't that it, Mr. Crouch? There.

ARNOLD. Oh, yes. So it is. I'm terribly sorry. (*He opens it out. Janie rises and takes it*.)

JANIE. Oh Harry, darling. Isn't it the most devastatingly lovely thing you've ever seen?

MISS TIPDALE. (*Adoringly*.) Mr. Crouch designed it, you know.

JANIE. Don't you find it affects you handling these divine furs all the time?

ARNOLD. Well, I'm sometimes troubled with little bits of fluff. (*Looks at Harry*.) In the nose and the throat!

HARRY. (*Angrily*.) You really are wasting my time, you know.

MISS TIPDALE. I'll get our girl to come and model it for you.

HARRY. There's no need for that. Slip it on, Janie.

JANIE. No, I want to see it for myself.

HARRY. (*To Miss Tipdale*.) You put it on, will you?

MISS TIPDALE. But I'm not the same shape as your wife.

HARRY. Well, somebody put it on!

16

ARNOLD. (*To Harry.*) Shall I or will you? (*Harry gives him a look.*) I'll ring for Miss Whittington.

HARRY. Never mind. (*To Miss Tipdale.*) You put it on. (*She does so, and looks vaguely uncomfortable in it.*)

JANIE. Oh Harry, darling, isn't it the most gorgeous colour? (*To Miss Tipdale.*) And it must be so warm.

MISS TIPDALE. (*Ecstatically.*) It's the most lovely thing I've ever seen.

HARRY. (*Non-committally.*) Yes, well—I don't know.

ARNOLD. (*With pride.*) You don't know!? D'you mean to say you can stand there viewing this unique achievement and then express some doubt as to its supreme merit, when every single tiny hair on it cries out "perfection"!

HARRY. All I said was I don't know.

ARNOLD. Then allow me to tell you, Mr. McMichael, that I know the pedigree of each pelt personally and each one is chosen for its size, colour and texture so that—

HARRY. I'm a very busy man. (*Looks at his watch.*) I have to get back to the office.

ARNOLD. Yes of course. Have you got your car with you?

HARRY. No, I always use taxis.

ARNOLD. (*Calls.*) Taxi! Miss Tipdale, get a taxi, please.

MISS TIPDALE. Yes, Mr. Crouch. (*Starts to go.*)

JANIE. I'll put it on now. (*She does so. Miss Tipdale goes, leaving door open.*)

ARNOLD. It looks even more beautiful on you, Mrs. McMichael.

JANIE. Thank you. And it's such a fantastic bargain at five hundred.

ARNOLD. Yes, fantastic is the word, isn't it? Do you know, sir, that each pelt in that coat comes from an exclusive breed of female Canadian wild mink and these are bred in only one square mile of Northern Alberta. In short this is one of the most valuable coats we've ever had.

HARRY. Then why is it only five hundred pounds?

ARNOLD. That's a very interesting point. But I won't bore you with the explanation.   •

HARRY. Try me.

ARNOLD. No—I assure you, it wouldn't interest the layman.

HARRY. Oh, I know a little bit about furs.

ARNOLD. (*Nonplussed.*) Oh. Not so much a layman after all.

17

(*Stalling for time.*) How about you, are you a good lay, madam—er—good lay woman, madam.

HARRY. (*Finally.*) Now look here— What about the price?

ARNOLD. Won't accept a penny less than five hundred.

HARRY. Why is it going cheap?

ARNOLD. Is it? I didn't hear anything. (*Puts his ear to the coat.*)

HARRY. God! (*To Janie.*) Come on, let's go. (*Mr. Frencham enters from* u. l. *leaving door open and along rostrum to* c. *followed by Miss Tipdale.*)

MR. FRENCHAM. Oh, blast! don't say I've missed her again.

MISS TIPDALE. She's taken the stairs. I believe the doorman is guarding a meter for you.

MR. FRENCHAM. That's no use now. Tell her I've gone to Chelsea Police Station.

MISS TIPDALE. Yes. Shall I say why?

MR. FRENCHAM. Damn car's been towed away. (*He exits* u. l.)

HARRY. We're going too.

JANIE. But Harry, the mink. Don't look a gift horse in the mouth.

HARRY. I've had enough.

JANIE. But, Harry, you promised—

HARRY. I promised nothing. (*Turns to go.*)

ARNOLD. Please, Mr. McMichael, we must have something that would interest you. I've got an ocelot, I've got a leopard, I've got a beaver.

MISS TIPDALE. (*Enters.*) I've got a taxi.

HARRY. Thank God for that, I've had enough of this place.

JANIE. But, Harry darling, you haven't bought the mink.

HARRY. No and I'm not going to. See you later.

ARNOLD. Please don't go. I tell you what. Perhaps you'd care to see my latest mole.

HARRY. My God! (*He exits with Miss Tipdale. There is a pause.*)

JANIE. (*To Arnold, sweetly.*) Well done, darling.

ARNOLD. Thank you. (*Gilbert enters, fuming.*)

GILBERT. Cretinous Crouch. What have you done? What have you done?

ARNOLD. Nothing.

GILBERT. Nothing? You've ruined everything.

ARNOLD. I did my best, Bodley.

GILBERT. (*To audience.*) Best?! (*To Janie.*) Janie, my proud beauty—what can I say? I'm abject, desolate, undone.

JANIE. (*Gently.*) It was just one of those things.

GILBERT. It was sheer disaster. Crouch handled the whole thing like a fumbling three year old.

JANIE. No, Poppet. It could have happened to anyone.

GILBERT. (*Slightly surprised.*) I must say you're taking it remarkably well.

JANIE. As Mr. Crouch said, he did his best.

ARNOLD. Yes.

GILBERT. Shut up, Crouch!

JANIE. Now don't ruffle yourself, Gilbert.

GILBERT. What a sweet, kind, understanding woman you are.

JANIE. Of course.

GILBERT. (*To Arnold.*) Crouch, have you ever met such a sweet, kind, understanding woman?

ARNOLD. Well, there was one occasion when I was camping in Cornwall.

GILBERT. Take it from me, my darling, he hasn't. Now. I'm sorry about this little contretemps, but I'll make it up in some other way before tonight.

JANIE. All right. (*She gives him a kiss.*)

GILBERT. Not in front of Crouch. We'll have to doctor his afternoon tea.

JANIE. Goodbye, darling. Goodbye, Arnie. (*She moves towards the door u. l.*)

GILBERT. Er—one tiny moment, beloved.

JANIE. (*Turning.*) Mm?

GILBERT. You've—er—forgotten the coat.

JANIE. No, I haven't. Goodbye. (*She moves to go again.*)

GILBERT. Beloved, believe me—it's still adorning your graceful shoulders.

JANIE. Can you think of a better place for it? (*Simply.*) Gillie, you promised it to me.

ARNOLD. I don't know what to say!

GILBERT. Shut up, Crouch! (*To Janie.*) My angel, you must realise that the status quo has suffered a minor catastrophe.

JANIE. You promised me the coat, Gillie. I'm going to have it.

ARNOLD. I think you're to have a bit of trouble, Mr. Bodley!

GILBERT. Shut up, Crouch! (*To Janie.*) You must see, Janie, that

19

for you to become the proud possessor of this coat is now fraught with difficulties of elephantine proportions.

JANIE. I see no difficulty. I simply walk out through the door.

GILBERT. What do you say when you come face to face with your husband?

JANIE. Hello, Harry, look what Gillie gave me. (*Gilbert stands there aghast.*)

GILBERT. But if you tell Harry I gave it you he'll—he'll think—he'll. *know*—well he'll *think* he knows that I—I—I—I—I— (*To Arnold.*) Crouch, say something.

ARNOLD. I pass.

GILBERT. Janie, was it not you, yourself, who said you had no wish to hurt Harry's feelings?

JANIE. Ah, that was before I knew how stingy he was (*Vamping him.*) Now, how much was my Gilly Willy prepared to pay towards this coat?

GILBERT. Er—

JANIE. Four and a half thousand.

GILBERT. True.

JANIE. (*With arm round him.*) And that was just for an outside chance in the distant future.

GILBERT. (*On edge.*) Well, I wouldn't put it like that—

JANIE. And Harry wouldn't even pay five hundred.

ARNOLD. For a sure thing every night. (*They both look at him.*) Would it be better if I retired?

GILBERT. It heads the agenda for the next meeting.

JANIE. Goodbye, darling. (*Moves to go.*)

GILBERT. Stop. You are not going with that coat.

JANIE. Well, I'm not going without it.

GILBERT. You are not leaving the building!

JANIE. (*Capitulating.*) All right. If you say so, my darling. I will stay with pleasure. (*She poses seductively on the couch. Gilbert and Arnold look apprehensively at each other.*)

GILBERT. Janie, the coat and no more of your nonsense. I am not to be put upon.

JANIE. I shall stay here until I get my own way.

ARNOLD. Oh dear.

GILBERT. Crouch! A fruitless attitude.

JANIE. You think so?

GILBERT. The customers will call as usual and will see nothing untoward in a pretty girl sitting on a couch. (*Janie removes the coat.*) So stay as long as you like, that is if you don't mind being ignored. (*Throughout the ensuing speech, Janie removes her dress and stockings and stands there in bra, panties and shoes.*)

ARNOLD. Ah!

GILBERT. Will you be quiet!

ARNOLD. I was only going to say—

GILBERT. Not another word. We men don't give way to feminine blackmail. In the course of a varied and I may add, not uninteresting life, many women have tried to score off Gilbert Bodley. None I'm proud to say have so far succeeded. (*Arnold turns and does a double-take on seeing Janie in a stripper's pose. He becomes extremely agitated and tries to attract Gilbert's attention by miming a strip-tease act. Gilbert brushes him off.*) I know I may sound hard and cynical, Arnold, but firmness is the only answer to a woman's wiles. Come along, Crouch, business as usual. (*Still not seeing Janie, he goes to the telephone and lifts the receiver.*) Tippers. Miss Tipdale, come along, where are you? Let's have a little speed and efficiency. (*Arnold is tugging at his sleeve.*) Desist, Crouch. (*In phone.*) Is anybody there? One knock for yes and two knocks for no— Ah there you are. Is there anything I should be looking into? (*Arnold nods furiously and points at Janie.*) . . . . Oh yes . . . well a brief note I think should suffice . . . take this down. "Dear Lady Dixon . . ." (*He suddenly sees Janie.*) Strewth!! (*Bangs the receiver down.*) Your clothes, Janie! For God's sake do something!

JANIE. All right, darling. (*She deliberately walks to the window and tosses them out.*)

GILBERT. Janie! What are you doing?

JANIE. Nothing, darling, just going home. Goodbye, Arnie. (*She walks towards the door* U. L.)

ARNOLD. Stop her, Mr. Bodley.

GILBERT. Janie!! (*Janie gets to the door. They both dive to stop her.*)

JANIE. But I thought you wanted me to go without the coat.

ARNOLD. Come away from that draughty keyhole. (*There is a knock at the door. Arnold grabs the mink and throws it over her shoulders. In doing this Arnold gets his hand underneath the coat and on Janie's bosom.*)

GILBERT. Who is it? Who is it?

MISS TIPDALE. (*Off.*) Miss Tipdale.

GILBERT. You can't come in.

MISS TIPDALE. (*Enters, leaving door open.*) I beg your pardon. (*She stops short on seeing Arnold's hand under Janie's coat. With a horrified look on his face Arnold slowly removes his arm. Miss Tipdale has notebook in her hand.*)

GILBERT. (*After a pause.*) What d'you want? What d'you want?

MISS TIPDALE. We were cut off, weren't we?

GILBERT. (*Not understanding.*) I should hardly think so.

MISS TIPDALE. But Lady Dixon's letter.

GILBERT. Well, open it, open it.

MISS TIPDALE. No, you were corresponding with her.

GILBERT. With a woman of eighty? Now get out, Tippers!

MISS TIPDALE. But is this all you wish to say to the lady?

GILBERT. What?

MISS TIPDALE. "Dear Lady Dixon—strewth!"

GILBERT. It's brief and to the point.

MISS TIPDALE. Isn't the language a little strong for Lady Dixon?

GILBERT. It's lucky for her it wasn't a damn sight stronger. Now get out, Tippers! (*Miss Tipdale is bustled out by Gilbert who closes door. Gilbert turns to Janie.*) Now, Janie, I am prepared to overlook everything if you'll be reasonable and go. (*In answer Janie seductively pulls out her undone bra from inside the fur coat and then calmly steps out of her panties. She holds the panties in one hand and the bra in the other. Gilbert is stunned as Janie walks to the open window and tosses both bra and panties out. Arnold rushes to Gilbert in terror.*) Janie! Are you bereft of all—

ARNOLD. Indeed she is.

GILBERT. Crouch! (*To Janie.*) You're raving mad.

ARNOLD. Stark raving.

GILBERT. Crouch! Janie! For heaven's sake, show us a little pity!

ARNOLD. No, don't show us that—

GILBERT. (*Forestalling Arnold.*) Crouch! (*Janie sits sexily on the couch and crosses her legs. Gilbert and Arnold, open-mouthed, are relieved that nothing further is revealed.*)

JANIE. Do I detect a note of panic creeping into that hard cynical firmness?

GILBERT. Panic? Never. Just a touch of sheer terror. Come along, Janie, I'll retrieve your garments. Then as Shakespeare said, "put your clothes on and go home."

ARNOLD. I don't think he did.

GILBERT. Who? Did what?

ARNOLD. Shakespeare, say "put your clothes on and go home."

GILBERT. He must have. We've all said it. (*Arnold ponders this.*)

ARNOLD. I haven't.

GILBERT. (*Turns angrily.*) Stop arguing! Do something. Get her off the couch, Crouch. (*There is a knock at the door. Gilbert and Arnold quickly sit either side of her. Arnold wraps the collar firmly around Janie and, in doing so, his hand inadvertently goes under the coat once more. Miss Tipdale enters and again stops short on seeing Arnold's hand under the coat. Arnold slowly takes his hand out. At the last moment his hand shakes and he hurriedly rests it on his leg.*) What is it, Tippers? Can't you find something better to do than fly in and out of that door? (*Miss Tipdale looks at the three of them with growing suspicion.*)

MISS TIPDALE. It's Phillips, the doorman.

GILBERT. What about him?

MISS TIPDALE. He's rung up from downstairs.

GILBERT. Splendid. If anything else startling occurs during the day, don't hesitate to let us know.

MISS TIPDALE. He's just seen some woman's clothes falling down.

GILBERT. Phillips is having quite a day, isn't he?

MISS TIPDALE. He thinks they came from this direction. A dress and stockings.

ARNOLD. What about underwear?

MISS TIPDALE. Underwear?

ARNOLD. No, it's all right. I suppose they take longer to land.

GILBERT. Why? (*Arnold mimes a bra floating down.*) Have you finished, Crouch?

ARNOLD. Yes.

GILBERT. You'd better bring them inside, Miss Tipdale. It looks bad.

MISS TIPDALE. I'm afraid I can't.

GILBERT. Why not?

MISS TIPDALE. They've landed on top of a number 9 bus and they've gone off.

GILBERT. Where to?

MISS TIPDALE. Westminster Abbey.

GILBERT. God!

23

ARNOLD. I never knew the number 9 bus went past the front door. I always get the tube to Tottenham Court Road and—

GILBERT. Quiet. (*The intercom phone rings. Miss Tipdale lifts the receiver and speaks.*)

MISS TIPDALE. (*On phone.*) Salon, here . . . Oh. Yes, Phillips . . . . I see . . . Thank you. (*She puts the receiver down and turns to them.*) The underwear's landed.

GILBERT. Incredible.

MISS TIPDALE. Yes, he's positive it's fallen from this direction.

GILBERT. That's quite ridiculous. Don't you agree, Crouch?

ARNOLD. Oh, quite. I've never seen a fallen woman's underwear.

GILBERT. Be that as it may. (*To Miss Tipdale.*) Retrieve them. You never know, they may fit one of us.

MISS TIPDALE. That's impossible.

GILBERT. (*With a laugh.*) Ah, we could always have them let out.

MISS TIPDALE. No, what I mean, Mr. Bodley, is they're irretrievable.

GILBERT. How so?

MISS TIPDALE. The underwear has caught up on the minute hand of our clock. . . .

GILBERT. God, how I suffer! Not a very good advertisement, Miss Tipdale. Get them off at once. (*He pushes off a bewildered Miss Tipdale who shuts the door.*)

JANIE. Are you ready to give in yet, Gillie?

GILBERT. Never! (*There is a knock at the door. Gilbert and Arnold fly to either side of Janie, hastily rearrange the fur on her and look innocent. Arnold, without thinking, goes to put his hand under Janie's coat. Gilbert slaps it. Miss Tipdale enters as Arnold is shaking his hand and leaves door open.*)

MISS TIPDALE. Excuse me, Mr. Bodley—

GILBERT. You're popping in and out of that door like a demented cuckoo.

MISS TIPDALE. (*Slightly put out.*) Well, I just thought Madam would like to know that Mr. McMichael has returned.

ARNOLD. How marvellous.

GILBERT. How terrible!

ARNOLD. How terrible!

GILBERT. (*To Janie.*) Now, I hope you're satisfied. Quickly, into the storeroom. (*He opens the door D. R. and pushes her off, leav-*

ing the door ajar. Janie takes her bag with her.) Crouch, you're in charge.

ARNOLD. I flatly refuse—

GILBERT. Shut up. Miss Tipdale, are you prepared to lend a hand in our time of need?

ARNOLD. Mr. Bodley, you can't possibly involve Miss Tipdale in your erotic intrigue.

GILBERT. Let the lady speak for herself. (*To Miss Tipdale.*) May I involve you in my erotic intrigue?

MISS TIPDALE. Well, I'm prepared to go so far, and no further.

GILBERT. Bear that in mind, Crouch. (*To Miss Tipdale.*) Show Mr. McMichael in.

JANIE. (*Opening door.*) What about my underwear?

GILBERT. Show that in, too. (*He pushes Janie out through door* D. R., *and then follows her in and shuts door.*)

ARNOLD. No, no, please. I'm not up to it. (*Arnold crosses to door and grabs the handle. It is locked. Arnold is once again struggling with the door handle as Harry enters through door* U. L., *leaving it open.*)

HARRY. How much longer do you—? (*He stops on seeing Arnold in the same position at the door. Arnold smiles foolishly at him.*)

ARNOLD. Yes, that's locked. Still locked. Make a note of that, will you, Miss Tipdale. Door still locked at 12.28. (*Harry gives him a "deadpan" look.*)

HARRY. Look here, has my wife gone?

ARNOLD. Oh, yes, very. She's been gone a long time. When did she last go, Miss Tipdale?

MISS TIPDALE. (*To Harry.*) I think she left when you did, virtually.

ARNOLD. (*Quickly.*) Yes. She was as virtual when she left as when she came.

HARRY. (*Slightly confused.*) What?

ARNOLD. We made a note of it, didn't we?

MISS TIPDALE. If you'll excuse me, Mr. Crouch, I'll just go and see to that other matter.

ARNOLD. No, I think I'd prefer you to stay, please.

MISS TIPDALE. Don't you want me to see about the things on the clock?

ARNOLD. On the clock?

MISS TIPDALE. The little things dangling from the minute hand.

25

ARNOLD. (*Looks at watch.*) I shouldn't worry, Miss Tipdale. It's nearly 12.30, and when it is, they'll drop off. (*He mimes them dropping off the hand.*)

MISS TIPDALE. Oh. (*As Miss Tipdale exits* U. L. *Mrs. Frencham enters, leaving door open.*)

MRS. FRENCHAM. Miss Tipdale . . .

MISS TIPDALE. Not now, madam. (*She goes.*)

ARNOLD. (*Picking up her ocelot.*) Oh, Mrs. Frencham—there hasn't been a moment to brush it.

MRS. FRENCHAM. Have you seen my husband?

ARNOLD. Yes. Now it's all right. He's at Chelsea Police Station.

MRS. FRENCHAM. Chelsea Police Station?!

ARNOLD. Yes, he was committing a minor offense in the street.

MRS. FRENCHAM. George! (*She puts a hand to her brow and exits, leaving door open.*)

HARRY. (*Impatiently.*) Now look here, Mr.—er—er—er—

ARNOLD. —Er—

HARRY. Crouch.

ARNOLD. Thank you—I had it right on the tip of my tongue.

HARRY. I'm a very busy man, and I haven't time to beat about the bush.

ARNOLD. Oh, what a shame.

HARRY. Well now, about this business—

ARNOLD. (*Nervously.*) Business?

HARRY. The mink.

ARNOLD. (*Delighted.*) Oh, the mink?

HARRY. Yes, the mink.

ARNOLD. Nothing else?

HARRY. (*Frowning.*) No.

ARNOLD. The coat, the whole coat and nothing but the coat?

HARRY. What else?

ARNOLD. What else—yes!

HARRY. I've been thinking it over and I've decided to change my mind.

ARNOLD. Oh, Mr. McMichael, I can't tell you how thrilled I am!

HARRY. Good.

ARNOLD. I'll get the coat immediately. Now, where—ah yes. (*He comes to the door* D. R. *but it's locked. He hesitates, remem-*

26

bering that Harry's wife is naked in there. Loudly for Gilbert's benefit.) So you've changed your mind, Mr. McMichael?

HARRY. (*Flinching slightly.*) Yes.

ARNOLD. (*When the door doesn't open, shouting.*) Changed your mind about the mink, Mr. McMichael.

HARRY. (*Eyeing him.*) Yes.

ARNOLD. (*Shouting.*) Good. You shall have it at once. Mr. McMichael. The *mink*, Mr. McMichael. (*Bangs door. The door opens and Gilbert enters brightly with the mink.*)

GILBERT. 'Morning, Crouch. 'Morning, Sir. (*He hands Arnold the mink and goes straight back into the storeroom.*)

ARNOLD. How's that for service? (*Gilbert having seen the nude Janie comes rushing back on, grabs the ocelot from Arnold, slings it through the door and shuts it.*) This is Mr. Bodley, our Managing Director.

GILBERT. How do you do?

HARRY. Ah, Mr. Bodley. My wife has met you, I think.

GILBERT. Yes.

HARRY. But I haven't had the pleasure.

GILBERT. (*Pointedly.*) Neither have I. (*Harry frowns and looks at Arnold. Arnold tries to laugh.*)

HARRY. Five hundred I think you said the price was? (*Gilbert puts his arms around Harry's shoulders.*)

GILBERT. Indeed it was, dear, dear, dear Mr. McMichael.

HARRY. (*To Arnold.*) I never realised how much selling a coat meant to you fellows.

ARNOLD. Oh, yes. We become personally involved with our customers. (*Looking at Gilbert.*) Some of us more than others. (*Harry takes out an enormous wad of £10 notes.*)

HARRY. Five hundred. And I want a receipt. (*Harry moves to table to count out the money and sits chair R. of table.*)

ARNOLD. Certainly. Our cashier will give you one. (*Miss Tipdale enters door U. L. leaving it open.*)

MISS TIPDALE. Excuse me, Mr. Bodley—

GILBERT. Ah, Miss Tipdale! Have you got those things off the clock yet?

MISS TIPDALE. No, I'm afraid not.

GILBERT. Why not?

MISS TIPDALE. A gust of wind blew them onto the roof of a passing taxi. (*Gilbert looks at the audience in disbelief.*) But I've

27

phoned through to the boutique next door, and they're sending some up.

GILBERT. Get it right away.

MISS TIPDALE. There is one other thing, Mr. Bodley.

GILBERT. What is it?

MISS TIPDALE. A Mrs. Lawson is outside.

GILBERT. Mrs. Lawson? (*Harry looks up from counting the money.*)

HARRY. That's my secretary. Send her in.

MISS TIPDALE. (*Calling off.*) This way please, Mrs. Lawson. (*Miss Tipdale exits as Sue Lawson enters. She is a short cuddly blonde baggage about 23. Nothing up top but everything to make up for it elsewhere.*)

SUE. I got your message to meet you here, Mr. McMichael.

HARRY. Yes, that's right. Just try this on for size, my darling. (*He drapes the coat over her shoulders. Arnold and Gilbert gape at each other in horror as the full implication dawns on them.*)

SUE. (*Snuggling in coat.*) Oh! Oh!

ARNOLD. (*To audience.*) Oh, what a tangled web we weave—

GILBERT. Oh, shut up.

SUE. Oh, it's lovely, Mr. McMichael. (*She emits a silly giggle.*) You shouldn't have.

GILBERT AND ARNOLD. (*Together to audience.*) No, he shouldn't have.

HARRY. (*To Sue.*) You like it then, do you?

SUE. Mr. McMichael. (*She giggles.*) I don't know how to thank you.

ARNOLD. He'll think of something.

HARRY. It's a present for being a very good girl. (*Harry goes back to chair R. of table and sits counting out the £500. Arnold and Gilbert are left dumbfounded.*)

ARNOLD. (*Quietly to Gilbert.*) It certainly pays to be a good girl these days. (*Sue is admiring herself.*)

GILBERT. Have you any other interesting observations to make?

ARNOLD. Yes. I'll bet this is the first time you've spent four-and-a-half thousand pounds on someone else's mistress.

GILBERT. Good God, he can't get away with this! Crouch, get the champagne round. (*Arnold goes into the cocktail bar D. L. having taken 3 glasses from top and one bottle from freezer. Door D. L. left open.*)

SUE. Oh, champagne!

HARRY. No, we're in a hurry.

SUE. Oh, I'd do anything for champagne.

GILBERT. (*To Harry.*) You still say "no"?

HARRY. Well, perhaps just a quick one then. Here's your 500.

GILBERT. (*Not taking it.*) Now it's funny you should mention that, Mr. McMichael. Now what would your reaction be if I told you that I'd made a teensy-weensy mistake—now, you might say I said that coat would be £500.

HARRY. You did.

GILBERT. Did I? Ah, now that might be my teensy-weensy mistake. Now just supposing that I'd mislaid a zero. What would you say?

HARRY. I'd say "What the hell are you talking about?"

GILBERT. (*Laughs.*) Yes, I thought you might! (*Then, to audience.*) I feel ill. (*Arnold arrives with tray and three glasses of champagne leaving door* D. L. *open.*)

ARNOLD. Here we are, Mr. Bodley.

GILBERT. Ah! Get the glasses round, Arnold, will you please. (*Arnold does so.*) I always think business should be mixed with a modicum of pleasure, don't you? I think you might join us, Arnold.

ARNOLD. Well, I don't drink normally. (*Arnold goes to cocktail bar with tray.*)

GILBERT. (*With false gaiety.*) No. Usually on all fours out of a saucer. (*He laughs. Arnold gives him a look and exits.*)

SUE. I don't get it.

GILBERT. You will. (*Arnold has returned with a glass of champagne.*) Well, to coin a phrase—"Cheers." (*The men drink.*)

SUE. May all our troubles be little ones. (*The men splutter.*)

GILBERT. To return to the case of the missing zero— I just want to bring to your notice a mere trifle, a mere petite chose, a mere poco poco.

HARRY. What are you drivelling on about?

GILBERT. (*To audience.*) I wish I knew.

HARRY. (*To Arnold.*) There's your 500. Take it. (*Arnold does.*) Thanks for the drink.

GILBERT. Mr. McMichael! If I told you that coat might be worth 5,000 what would you say?

HARRY. I wouldn't say anything, I'd be too busy laughing.

29

ARNOLD. Oh, that's very good. (*Arnold laughs, Sue joins in. Gilbert looks at the audience for sympathy.*)

HARRY. Let me put it another way. The deal's done.

ARNOLD. No, don't put it another way! (*Miss Tipdale enters. She is carrying a paper bag, from an exclusive boutique.*)

MISS TIPDALE. Excuse me, Mr. Bodley, I think I've got just what you want.

GILBERT. Good. Let me pull the trigger!

MISS TIPDALE. It's for, "you know," in there. (*She quickly shows him the contents and shuts it again.*)

SUE. You know?

ARNOLD. Mr. Bodley's bird.

HARRY. Your bird?

GILBERT. Yes. My parrot actually.

ARNOLD. This is "you know's" lunch. (*Arnold takes the carrier bag.*)

HARRY. (*To Miss Tipdale.*) Look, miss, would you mind getting me a taxi?

MISS TIPDALE. Certainly, sir.

HARRY. I've wasted enough time here already. (*Miss Tipdale exits.*)

ARNOLD. I'll just give this to you know. (*He moves to the storeroom door.*)

GILBERT. (*Shouting.*) NO! Wait till our guests have gone.

SUE. Oh, let me see her.

GILBERT. Don't open the door, she's moulting.

SUE. I love parrots.

GILBERT. She's having a rest before lunch.

SUE. Oh, I'd love to feed her.

ARNOLD. No.

GILBERT. She won't be hungry yet. She had a very late breakfast.

SUE. Please!

ARNOLD. We'll feed it to the pigeons instead.

SUE. Lovely. Let me. (*She takes the bag from Arnold who hangs onto it.*)

ARNOLD. No. Don't pull it.

SUE. Please! (*They are struggling with bag.*)

GILBERT. (*Gilbert takes bag.*) Do you mind not interfering with our domestic arrangements?

30

HARRY. (*Harry takes bag.*) Do you mind not interfering with my secretary? If she wants to feed them, let her. (*Harry gives the bag to Sue.*)

ARNOLD. (*Snatches the bag.*) Come and get it! (*Arnold goes up steps R.—to windows C. Opens them and tips the contents straight out of the window. Yelling.*) Stop that bus!

SUE. Mr. Crouch! What is it?

GILBERT. Too late. They've flown off.

SUE. Oh, that was quick.

ARNOLD. (*Turning from window.*) Yes, they don't hang about those number nines.

HARRY. (*To Sue.*) Come on, Sue, let's go.

ARNOLD. One moment, pray.

GILBERT. It's worth a try. Let's both pray. (*Drops on his knees.*)

SUE. Are you feeling all right, Mr. Bodley?

GILBERT. Far from it. (*Gilbert gets up again.*)

ARNOLD. No, Mr. Bodley, at a time like this, the only solution is to bare one's breast. Don't you agree, Mrs.— (*He pulls up short.*) You see, there has been a very grave miscarriage of price tags here.

GILBERT. It's hopeless, Crouch.

ARNOLD. No, Mr. Bodley. You see we have sold Mr. McMichael this coat for £500 when in actual fact—

HARRY. If you're going to tell me it's worth five thousand, you can whistle for it. (*Gilbert whistles.*)

ARNOLD. In actual fact it is worth a mere £100.

HARRY AND GILBERT. What?

ARNOLD. Yes. That is nothing more than dyed rabbit.

HARRY. Now, just a minute. What are you trying to pull?

ARNOLD. Nothing, I assure you.

HARRY. I think I'm entitled to an explanation. I'm in the dark.

GILBERT. And I'm right there with you. Come on, Crouch.

ARNOLD. Very well. Seated one day in the storeroom, I was weary and—

GILBERT. Tell it, don't sing it.

ARNOLD. —I had two coats side by side. One was the genuine mink—the other, this rotten, old dyed rabbit. Are you with me?

GILBERT. No, not quite.

ARNOLD. Well, in the half-light of the storeroom I inadvertently got the price tags the wrong way round. (*There is a slight pause as they all take this in. Gilbert starts to smile.*)

31

SUE. D'you mean this isn't a genuine mink?

ARNOLD. No, I'm afraid not. The resemblance between mink and this rotten old lump of dyed rabbit is quite striking but superficial.

SUE. Oh, Harry.

ARNOLD. Don't you like it?

HARRY. It looks like the genuine article and that's all that matters. (*To Sue.*) Agreed?

SUE. Well, I mean, you did promise me a real one.

HARRY. Who's to know?

ARNOLD. Mr. McMichael, a genuine mink will always have about it an air of unrestrained flamboyance whereas this very soon looks an anxious and frightened thing. (*They all look at the coat.*)

HARRY. (*Getting angry.*) So why didn't you trot out a few of these facts earlier?

GILBERT. We're at fault. We freely admit it. It wasn't until Crouch saw the lining that the hideous truth struck home.

SUE. (*Taking coat off.*) Lining?

GILBERT. (*Takes coat from her.*) Yes.

HARRY. What's wrong with it?

GILBERT. What's wrong with what?

HARRY. The lining.

GILBERT. Ah, you may well ask.

HARRY. I do ask.

GILBERT. Crouch, tell him.

ARNOLD. I thought I'd finished.

HARRY. What's wrong with the lining? It looks perfect.

ARNOLD. That's the trouble. It'll outlast the coat. (*Miss Tipdale enters from door* U. L.—*leaving it open.*)

MISS TIPDALE. Excuse me, Mr. Bodley.

GILBERT. Not now, Tippers, please!

MISS TIPDALE. Mr. McMichael's taxi.

HARRY. Ah yes, I'll be there in a minute. (*To Arnold.*) Now then, you tell me that this bundle of rubbish is worthless.

ARNOLD. A mere one hundred pounds.

HARRY. Then give me back my 500.

ARNOLD. Certainly. (*Takes notes out of his pocket and gives them to Harry.*)

SUE. (*Disappointed.*) Oh, Harry.

32

HARRY. Shut up, angel! (*Turns his back on them and counts it quickly.*)

GILBERT. (*Surreptitiously shakes Arnold's hand. To Harry.*) If you should care to call and select another coat . . . don't hesitate to do so.

HARRY. Thank you very much, but I'm not interested in any other coat. You did say one hundred, didn't you? (*Thrusts £100 into Arnold's hand. He drapes mink over Sue and ushers her out. Gilbert and Arnold stare at each other open-mouthed.*)

MISS TIPDALE. Will there be anything else, Mr. Bodley?

GILBERT. God, I hope not.

ARNOLD. (*Rather dazed.*) When would you say things started to go wrong, Mr. Bodley?

GILBERT. (*Controlling his temper.*) Fourteen years ago, when you came to me straight from college—you walked through that door and you said— (*Janie enters* D. R., *still wearing Mrs. Frencham's ocelot, and stays by door.*)

JANIE. Gilbert, do you realise I've got no underclothes?

GILBERT. Or words to that effect.

MISS TIPDALE. Mrs. McMichael!

GILBERT. Get the lady her underclothes, Tippers.

MISS TIPDALE. But I did get them.

GILBERT. Well, get them again.

MISS TIPDALE. What happened to the last lot?

GILBERT. Need you ask?

JANIE. Well, what *did* happen?

ARNOLD. I fed them to the pigeons.

GILBERT. Ask a silly question.

JANIE. And who was that woman with Harry? (*Crouch and Bodley exchange a worried look.*)

GILBERT. Woman? What woman?

JANIE. Well, I was trying to listen through the door and it sounded like a woman.

GILBERT. No, no, there hasn't been a woman here, was there, Arnold? Only Miss Tipdale.

ARNOLD. Yes, she often sounds like a woman. (*Miss Tipdale reacts to this.*)

GILBERT. Don't stand there looking like a puzzled secretary, Tippers. Go and get a repeat order of lingerie. (*Miss Tipdale exits.*)

33

JANIE. Well, has Harry reconsidered and bought the mink for me?
ARNOLD. Yes.   GILBERT. No.
JANIE. What?
ARNOLD. No.   GILBERT. Yes.
JANIE. Well, which?
GILBERT. Neither, actually. I've just remembered. Crouch sent it to the cleaners.
ARNOLD. What?
JANIE. The cleaners? But it was brand new.
GILBERT. Ah, but he'd been mishandling it very badly.
JANIE. (*To Arnold.*) Is Gilbert telling me the truth?
GILBERT. (*Warningly.*) Crouch!
ARNOLD. (*Takes deep breath.*) Mrs. McMichael—in my opinion Mr. Bodley would not recognise the truth if it came in here at the top of a twenty foot pole and waggled in his face.
GILBERT. Don't listen to him! Janie, the only flower in my garden of love. The only star in my constellation of passion. The only— turn around, Crouch. (*Arnold does so.*) —the only promise of summer in, shall we say, the autumn of my life.
ARNOLD. Shall we say winter?
GILBERT. In the corner, Crouch. (*Arnold turns again.*) To tell you the truth, my darling, there has been a slight temporary hitch, but no matter—we can iron it out in bed tonight.
JANIE. Only if I've had my mink.
GILBERT. All I'm saying is that surely a mere mink won't jeopardise our journey to paradise.
JANIE. (*Sweetly.*) And all I'm saying is, if I don't get it, neither do you. (*Janie moves towards the balcony, going up* C. *steps. She stops and turns on top step.*)
GILBERT. Where are you going?
JANIE. Out onto the balcony. I'm merely going to stand there, open my coat wide and scream.
GILBERT. But that's ridiculous.
JANIE. No, darling, blackmail. (*She turns* U. *again, opens the French windows and goes out onto the balcony.*)
GILBERT. This is all your fault, Crouch.
ARNOLD. But she's not actually going to—
GILBERT. Of course not. (*Janie, with her back to the audience, calmly opens her coat wide and screams long and loud. Arnold and Gilbert are so shattered that they rush around like two de-*

34

mented idiots. *Finally they drag her back into the salon, holding her coat closed as Miss Tipdale from* U. L. *enters, leaving door open, she reacts as the perfect unruffled secretary. Arnold has sat Janie on the couch at* L. C. *end and then sits on her lap. Gilbert stands* L. *of them—holding Arnold's hand.*)

MISS TIPDALE. (*Calmly.*) Could I interrupt for a moment?

GILBERT. Can't you see we're busy? (*Gilbert, realising he's holding a man's hand, drops it.*)

ARNOLD. I'm not enjoying this, Miss Tipdale.

MISS TIPDALE. I think you ought to know that someone has just got out of a taxi.

GILBERT. I don't care.

MISS TIPDALE. Well, you ought to. It's your wife. (*Miss Tipdale exits* U. L. *on her line—leaving door open.*)

GILBERT. Yes, thank you— My wife! (*Gilbert then dashes up* C. *steps to door.*)

ARNOLD. (*In horror.*) Mrs. Bodley! (*Maude walks in briskly. Gilbert quickly embraces her and spins her round so that her back is to Arnold and Janie. Gilbert indicates to Arnold that he should take Janie into the storeroom* D. R. *Arnold is so terrified that he takes cover inside Janie's coat. Arnold and Janie worm their way into the storeroom, with Gilbert gesticulating madly. As soon as they're gone he spins Maude round again and gives her a smacking kiss.*)

GILBERT. Good to see you, Maude. (*Maude is nobody's fool. She is an attractive, businesslike woman of about 40 and is quite a sexy lady.*) God, it's good, Maude, it's really good to see you, Maude, good to see you, God, it's good, really good, Maude. Good to see.

MAUDE. (*Casually.*) Thank you, darling. What's on your mind?

GILBERT. Nothing! God, it's good to see you, Maude, really good. You're supposed to be in Monte Carlo!

MAUDE. Well, I discovered that a month is far too long to be without you.

GILBERT. Yes, I know exactly how you feel. (*Goes for the champagne.*) You're just in time for some champagne.

MAUDE. Oh, lovely, anything special to celebrate?

GILBERT. Er—since you mention it, no. We don't need anything special, for heaven's sake, do we? God, it's good to see you, Maude.

MAUDE. Yes, I think you said that before, darling.

GILBERT. Did I? Well, I'll say it again.

MAUDE. I'd rather you didn't.

GILBERT. (*Looks round.*) There ought to be a clean glass here somewhere.

MAUDE. What have you had, a party?

GILBERT. No, no, no—it was a sale actually.

MAUDE. Oh. Must have been a good one.

GILBERT. Indeed it was. Arnold and I pulled off something rather special.

MAUDE. Who is she?

GILBERT. God, it's good to see you, Maude.

MAUDE. Yes, but who?

GILBERT. We don't want to talk shop the moment you come in through the door, do we? Cheers!

MAUDE. Here's to you, my darling. And this is a small surprise present I've brought back for you. (*She hands him a stud box.*)

GILBERT. Oh, Maude, you shouldn't have. (*He starts to open it.*)

MAUDE. I couldn't resist it. Anyway, you know that whenever we've been parted for any length of time we like to give each other surprises.

GILBERT. Yes. (*Sees pin.*) Oh, it's beautiful.

MAUDE. Don't say you haven't got a surprise for me.

GILBERT. (*Shoots a glance at the storeroom. Then quickly.*) God, it's— So you couldn't wait to get back to me, eh?

MAUDE. No, all that sun and wine and all those lovely Frenchmen, if I'd stayed out there a moment longer I might have lost my head.

GILBERT. I'm a lucky man, Maude.

MAUDE. As long as you appreciate it.

GILBERT. Oh, I do. God, it's good to see you, Maude.

MAUDE. Well, what's been going on here?

GILBERT. Nothing, nothing at all, it's been as quiet as the grave. Do you know there hasn't been a woman in here since you left, Maude, would you believe it? That door has not opened to admit a woman for— I wouldn't mind for myself but it's the business I'm worried about— Not one woman, would you credit it?

MAUDE. But I thought you sold a coat this morning?

GILBERT. Yes, I did, but that was to a gentleman.

MAUDE. A gentleman?

36

GILBERT. He looked lovely in it. Sorry you've got to rush.

MAUDE. There's no rush, darling. Top it up for me, will you? (*She holds out glass.*)

GILBERT. That's my Maude. So, why did you come back?

MAUDE. Now, stop fishing, I've told you once. I missed you.

GILBERT. I missed you too.

MAUDE. Especially at night.

GILBERT. (*Filling his own glass.*) Me too.

MAUDE. I used to lie awake thinking about it.

GILBERT. Me too. Me too. (*Glancing at the storeroom door.*)

MAUDE. But we're all right now, aren't we?

GILBERT. (*Without thinking.*) You may be but I'm still— Yes, of course we are. It gives one a rosy glow just to think about it.

MAUDE. The champagne doesn't do any harm either.

GILBERT. I don't think I've ever felt more relaxed, more at ease with the world— (*Miss Tipdale enters door* U. L.—*leaving it open.*)

MISS TIPDALE. Do you still want me to get those things?

GILBERT. (*Whips round.*) Yes, and be quick about it, you old bat. (*Miss Tipdale exits.*)

MAUDE. Bat?

GILBERT. God, it's good to see you, Maude. What was I saying?

MAUDE. You were saying that you'd never felt so at ease with the world.

GILBERT. Yes.

MAUDE. What's Miss Tipdale gone for?

GILBERT. (*Looking at watch.*) No more than ten minutes, I hope. How're you feeling now, eh?

MAUDE. (*Slightly surprised.*) Fine, fine.

GILBERT. Yes, you're looking better. A little thinner in the face, perhaps.

MAUDE. I've put it on just about everywhere else.

GILBERT. (*Patting her bottom.*) No complaints. (*Maude gives a sexy chuckle.*)

MAUDE. Champagne's doing you good. Have some more.

GILBERT. I think it's time you went and said hello to the staff.

MAUDE. I said hello on the way in.

GILBERT. Good. Well, don't forget to say goodbye on the way out.

MAUDE. I'm not going yet.

GILBERT. Of course you are. You pop back to the flat and get the bed warm.

MAUDE. Darling!

GILBERT. That's what you've come back for, isn't it?

MAUDE. Not before lunch.

GILBERT. Oh, to hell with convention. I've got one or two bits of unfinished business, but I'll be with you in a jiffy.

MAUDE. If I'd known you felt like this I'd have come back yesterday.

GILBERT. Yes, that would have done it. (*Takes her glass.*) Off you go. I'll be as quick as I can. (*Kisses her and pushes her out* U. L. *Without thinking.*) And don't start without me. (*Calls.*) Come on, Crouch. All clear. No time to waste. (*Arnold enters from* D. R.)

ARNOLD. It's coming home to roost now, isn't it, Mr. Bodley?

GILBERT. Oh, shut up! Don't you understand, we have a crisis on our hands. Maude has come back two weeks early.

ARNOLD. I know that, but what for?

GILBERT. Never you mind. (*Janie enters from* D. R.)

JANIE. Gillie, I'll get claustrophobia in this poky place.

GILBERT. Forgive me, Janie, coat or no coat, our little rendezvous this evening will have to be postponed. Maude has come—Maude has gone. Maude's gone! (*Suddenly.*) Great Scott! (*He starts to march up and down in agony.*) I'm undone.

ARNOLD. What is it, Bodley?

GILBERT. Janie's underclothes.

ARNOLD. Miss Tipdale is organising that, surely?

GILBERT. Not those underclothes, you idiot. All those little frillies laid out in our room. My bed-warming present to Janie. Maude's on her way there now.

JANIE. Calm down, Gillie. With any luck your wife won't even notice them.

GILBERT. (*Explodes.*) Won't notice them?!

JANIE. No. She may not go into the bedroom.

GILBERT. That's exactly where she is going, hot foot.

JANIE. Gillie, you are working overtime.

GILBERT. If you'll only keep out of the way for five minutes. (*Takes her to door* R.)

38

JANIE. (*In doorway.*) It's damned chilly in there.

ARNOLD It'll be warming up pretty soon, I think. (*Gilbert pushes her in and shuts door.*)

GILBERT. I must get back to the flat before Maude. Get on to Miss Tipdale. You see if Tippers has got those underclothes yet.

ARNOLD. Very well, Mr. Bodley.

GILBERT. And when she brings the next lot in don't hand them straight over to London Transport. (*The intercom phone rings. They both rush to it but Arnold gets there first.*)

ARNOLD. (*On phone.*) Hello, hello.

GILBERT. (*Behind him.*) Who is it? Who is it?

ARNOLD. It's me. It's me.

GILBERT. On the other end.

ARNOLD. Oh, that's Miss Tipdale.

GILBERT. Good! Has she got the underclothes? (*He starts to go.*)

ARNOLD. No.

GILBERT. (*Stops.*) What do you mean, no?

ARNOLD. She says there's more trouble.

GILBERT. More trouble?

ARNOLD. (*To Gilbert.*) She came back unexpectedly.

GILBERT. Who did?

ARNOLD. Mrs. Bodley.

GILBERT. Maude? I know that, you nut.

ARNOLD. (*On phone.*) We know that, you nut—er—Miss Tipdale.

GILBERT. Tell her she's gone again.

ARNOLD. (*On phone.*) She's gone again. (*Gilbert starts to exit through door. To Gilbert:*) One moment, Mr. Bodley.

GILBERT. What is it now? (*He comes back to Arnold and stands L. of him.*)

ARNOLD. (*To Gilbert.*) She says she knows she went again but she's come back again.

GILBERT. D'you mean she's come back again again? (*Maude enters from door U. L. and along rostrum to L. C. She stands there, watching them.*)

ARNOLD. (*On phone.*) Do you mean she's come back again again? (*To Gilbert.*) She said . . . Yes, I think so. (*Arnold goes back to listening on the telephone.*)

GILBERT. No, that's impossible. (*He turns and sees Maude.*) Good Lord!

39

ARNOLD. (*On phone.*) Mr. Bodley said, "No, that's impossible" and then he said, "Good Lord!" (*Gilbert crosses to* L. *of Maude and is shaking her by the hand very formally. Arnold sits at table. On phone:*) No, start at the beginning, will you . . . She went away in the first place . . . Oh, came back in the first place. Yes . . . and now she's come back in the second place. . . . (*To Gilbert.*) Just a second. . . . (*During this Gilbert is nonchalantly tapping him on the shoulder to attract his attention to Maude.*) Oh, I see. And where is she now? . . . In our place. I'll tell him. (*To Gilbert.*) She says—that at the moment she's in . . . (*Seeing Maude.*) Ah! (*Rises. He madly tries to think of something to say. He puts the telephone receiver in his pocket and shakes her warmly by the hand as he speaks. Finally:*) God, it's good to see you, Mrs. Bodley.

MAUDE. Thank you, Arnold. It's good to see you, too.

ARNOLD. No. It must be much better for me to see you than it is for you to see me.

GILBERT. And don't stay away so long the next time, will you? How—er—did you find—er—find—things—er—at the flat?

MAUDE. Oh, I haven't been round there yet.

GILBERT. What a wise decision, Maude. (*To Arnold.*) Wasn't that a wise decision, Arnold?

ARNOLD. Definitely.

MAUDE. (*To Gilbert.*) Why?

GILBERT. (*To Arnold.*) Why?

ARNOLD. Why? Well, when you're away, Mrs. Bodley, it does get very dirty up there. (*Gilbert glares at him.*) I mean the flat gets dirty.

MAUDE. (*To Gilbert.*) But surely you've had Mrs. Ogden every morning.

GILBERT. It's a lie! I don't even know the woman.

ARNOLD. No, I believe Mrs. Ogden is your cleaning lady.

GILBERT. Yes, I believe she is. What a shocking suggestion, Maude. (*Miss Tipdale enters from door* L.)

MISS TIPDALE. Excuse me, Mr. Crouch, you've left the phone off.

ARNOLD. Oh, yes, so I have! (*Arnold looks for the receiver and is surprised to find it in his pocket. On phone.*) You were in my pocket, Miss Tipdale! That'll be all, Miss Tipdale—and don't forget to get those things.

MISS TIPDALE. Right away.

ARNOLD. (*On phone.*) Splendid girl. I'll see you later, goodbye. (*He puts the phone down, and turns to see Miss Tipdale. He reacts to her and the telephone.*) What do you want, Miss Tipdale?

MISS TIPDALE. Nothing.

ARNOLD. Well, take it and go. And get a move on. We've got a very busy day ahead. (*Miss Tipdale exits* U. L. *and closes door.*)

MAUDE. Arnold, how much did you have to drink at this party this morning?

GILBERT. What a damn good idea, Maude. Arnold, open another bottle of champagne, will you. I'll leave you two to discuss the autumn sales, while I pop back and hoover the flat.

MAUDE. It's unlike you to be so domestic, Gilbert.

GILBERT. Oh, I'm changing my ways, darling.

ARNOLD. (*To Gilbert.*) Not before time, darling.

GILBERT. Champagne, darling! (*Arnold is by door of cocktail cabinet and has opened it as Gilbert moves to* U. L. *door. Arnold exits—leaving door ajar.*)

MAUDE. Oh, before you go, Gilbert—

GILBERT. Yes, beloved?

MAUDE. Could you let me have some money?

GILBERT. Money?

MAUDE. That's what I came back for.

GILBERT. What do you want, change for the meter?

MAUDE. (*Laughing.*) No, I want to buy a couple of warm dresses. I wasn't expecting this weather.

GILBERT. Ah, I've only got a couple of fivers. Ask the cashier. (*Moves a pace or two to door.*)

MAUDE. But you must have more than that left.

GILBERT. Left—from what?

MAUDE. The four and a half thousand. (*Gilbert is frozen with horror. There is a crash of glasses from the cocktail cabinet and Arnold's head appears round the door. He creeps out and shuts it.*)

GILBERT. (*To Maude.*) Four and a half thousand?

MAUDE. (*Innocently.*) That you withdrew from the bank.

GILBERT. (*Nervously.*) From the bank?

MAUDE. This morning.

GILBERT. This morning?

MAUDE. Yes.

GILBERT. (*Broadly.*) Oh—that four and a half thousand.

41

MAUDE. Yes.

GILBERT. Ah! No, I haven't got any of that left. (*Sensing peril, Gilbert tries to laugh it off with Arnold. To Arnold:*) I can't keep anything from my little Maude, can I? Come on, Maude. How did you hear about it?

MAUDE. Ahh!

ARNOLD. (*Gleefully.*) Ah! Perhaps she had you tailed. (*Arnold laughs and Gilbert feels obliged to join in.*)

GILBERT. (*Laughing.*) She wouldn't do a thing like that— (*Gradually stops laughing.*) Would you?

MAUDE. As a matter of fact, my discovery was just a funny coincidence. (*She chuckles.*)

GILBERT. (*To Arnold.*) Ah, just a funny coincidence.

MAUDE. Yes, on the way back from the airport this morning I called in at the bank to deposit my few remaining francs.

GILBERT. Yes?

MAUDE. And, would you believe it, I had the same young man who'd cashed your cheque earlier.

GILBERT. (*In mock amazement.*) No.

MAUDE. Yes, the one with the teeth.

ARNOLD. Oh yes, he's always ready for a chat. You know the one.

GILBERT. (*Mentally strangling him.*) Yes, I know the one.

MAUDE. Well, you know how he can never bear to let you go without trying to be funny.

GILBERT. Mm.

ARNOLD. Yes, I shall never forget what he said to me the day the credit squeeze was announced.

GILBERT. Force yourself.

ARNOLD. No, it was much funnier than that.

GILBERT. Stop interrupting. I suppose old blabbermouth said, "When you see your husband ask him if he got home safely without being attacked by bandits."

MAUDE. (*Laughs.*) Yes, wasn't it funny?

GILBERT. Hilarious.

ARNOLD. Uproarious!

GILBERT. Crouch!—champagne.

MAUDE. Gilbert, I do believe you're blushing.

GILBERT. What would I have to blush about?

MAUDE. I don't know. Something to do with that money, maybe.

42

GILBERT. Oh, good Maude, Lord. That was nothing.

MAUDE. I'd hardly call four and a half thousand nothing. (*Arnold appears with two glasses of champagne.*)

GILBERT. I—I—I—I—just suddenly thought I'd take it out.

MAUDE. And spend it suddenly too.

GILBERT. No, I haven't. I haven't. I haven't. I haven't. (*Like a stuck needle.*)

MAUDE. All right, you haven't. (*Gilbert takes glass from Arnold.*)

GILBERT. That's what I said, I haven't I haven't I hav— (*Suddenly.*) I'll tell you what I did with it.

ARNOLD. (*To Gilbert.*) Stout fellow, Mr. Bodley.

GILBERT. Arnold borrowed it from me. (*Arnold's smile fades and he downs the glass of champagne which he is holding.*)

ARNOLD. (*Aghast.*) What are you saying, Mr. Bodley?

GILBERT. Do you deny you've got that money?

ARNOLD. Most emphatically!

MAUDE. He denies it.

GILBERT. I'm sorry. (*He opens Arnold's jacket.*)

ARNOLD. Take your hands off me.

GILBERT. Ah, so you *have* got it. (*Goes for his pocket again.*)

MAUDE. Arnold! (*Arnold hastily gathers up the notes.*)

ARNOLD. That's not my money. It's Mr. Bodley's money.

GILBERT. Then what's it doing in your pocket?

ARNOLD. You gave it to me.

GILBERT. Yes—as a loan.

ARNOLD. Mrs. Bodley! I feel you should know everything.

MAUDE. Well, if it's a personal matter I'd really rather not.

ARNOLD. No, I must speak.

GILBERT. NO! Please, Arnold, spare me that. The moment of truth has arrived. Maude is my wife. She shall hear the facts from me.

ARNOLD. The truth, the whole truth—

GILBERT. And nothing but. (*He takes deep breath.*) Please get the champagne, Arnold. I think Maude may need it.

ARNOLD. Very well, Mr. Bodley. (*Arnold goes into cocktail cabinet.*)

GILBERT. (*To Maude.*) Maude, I'm very much afraid that I've been keeping something from you for some time now. It's not pleasant. Loath as I am to admit it, women and even sex are involved.

MAUDE. Oh, Gilbert! (*Arnold reappears with two glasses of champagne, shuts door quietly and comes to L. of Gilbert.*)

GILBERT. No—no—please, hear me out. It's not a new story and it's now reached its unhappy but inevitable conclusion.

ARNOLD. Well said, Mr. Bodley.

GILBERT. Thank you. Where was I?

ARNOLD. The inevitable conclusion.

GILBERT. Blackmail has reared its ugly head—and the price is, as is not unknown on these occasions, a mink coat.

MAUDE. No! And that's what the money was for?

GILBERT. Yes. (*He hangs his head.*) Correct, Crouch?

ARNOLD. Correct, Mr. Bodley.

GILBERT. And that is how Arnold bought off Miss Tipdale. (*There is a pause as Arnold's sanctimonious smile crumbles. Maude is staring at Arnold, aghast. Arnold pours one glass of champagne into another and drinks it down. Gilbert "chalks" one up to himself.*)

MAUDE. Oh, Arnold, I'm so dreadfully sorry.

GILBERT. So am I.

ARNOLD. But it's not Miss Tipdale.

GILBERT. You cad, have you moved on to another one already?

ARNOLD. Certainly not!

GILBERT. I bet you, Maude, he's had women through here like buses.

ARNOLD. I never have! (*The door D. R. opens and Janie steps out, leaving door open.*)

JANIE. I'll catch my death of cold in here. (*She stops—aghast. She reacts on seeing Maude.*)

GILBERT. (*With studied casualness.*) This is our latest fur, Maude. Would you be so kind as to show my wife . . . ? (*To Janie. Janie walks to and fro "modelling" the coat.*) Charming. Absolutely charming. Don't you agree, Maude? Arnold's latest creation. You must be very proud of it, Arnold.

ARNOLD. (*Stammering.*) I—ah—ah—er—

GILBERT. Too overcome for words are you?

ARNOLD. Mm.

GILBERT. I do understand. Modesty forbids him. His artistry is as impeccable as ever, Maude, don't you agree?

MAUDE. Well, I wouldn't say it was a world beater.

GILBERT. No, very ordinary. Not one of your more inspired moments, Arnold. (*Gibberish from Arnold.*)

MAUDE. In fact, I seem to remember seeing that coat before I went away.

GILBERT. No, I know the one you mean, Maude. It was similar, but utterly different.

ARNOLD. I would like to say *here* and *now*—

GILBERT. And you said them very well, too. (*Arnold glares at Gilbert.*)

MAUDE. You know, Gilbert, I'm sure that's the same coat. Anyway, we can soon tell, can't we?

GILBERT. Can we—how?

MAUDE. By looking at the lining.

ARNOLD. Yes!

GILBERT. No!

ARNOLD. No!

GILBERT. (*To Janie.*) Thank you, Miss—er—

MAUDE. Wait a minute! Gilbert!

GILBERT. Yes, beloved?

MAUDE. I've never seen this girl before.

ARNOLD. (*Triumphantly.*) Ahh!

GILBERT. Haven't you?

MAUDE. She's not one of our models.

ARNOLD. Ahhh!

GILBERT. (*Looks closely.*) I do believe you're right.

MAUDE. Who are you, miss?

JANIE. I'm—

GILBERT. Oh, no, you're not.

ARNOLD. Oh, yes, she is!

GILBERT. Ah! So you admit it, do you? Another one of his girl friends!

ARNOLD. Mr. Bodley, may you be forgiven. (*To Janie.*) Will you kindly tell our Lady Chairman with whom you are associating. And be not afeared, because "Absolute truth belongs to thee alone."

GILBERT. (*Pulling Janie round.*) One moment—

ARNOLD. (*Pulling her back.*) No. Once and for all. I want the truth.

MAUDE. Come on then, let's have it.

GILBERT. Can't you see, he's trying to bluff his way out? He's

45

already given the girl a mink coat. (*Quickly.*) Or if she hasn't got it now she'll have it before tonight. (*Pointedly to Janie.*) And I'll bet that if she plays her cards right she'll get a second fur coat and a sports car for good measure.

MAUDE. Let the girl answer the question.

GILBERT. Certainly. What was the question?

ARNOLD. With whom are you associating?

JANIE. D'you want me to tell the truth?

ARNOLD. Of course I do.

JANIE. Leaving out nothing, Mr. Crouch?

ARNOLD. Nothing!

JANIE. Nothing, Arnold?

ARNOLD. (*With slight apprehension.*) Nothing.

JANIE. Are you sure, Arnie? (*One pace to Arnold.*)

ARNOLD. (*Swallowing.*) Yes, of course I'm sure.

JANIE. Well, if you say so—Arnie—Warnie. (*One more pace to him and she puts her arms around his neck.*)

ARNOLD. (*The words sticking in his throat.*) Yes—I—do.

MAUDE. (*Finally.*) Who is it?

ARNOLD. (*Almost crying.*) I think it must be me. (*Gilbert looks at the audience and "chalks" one up to himself.*)

MAUDE. (*To Janie.*) I would suggest, madam, that you leave our salon immediately and for you and Mr. Crouch to arrange your assignations elsewhere in future.

GILBERT. Hear, hear.

JANIE. I think I ought to stay.

MAUDE. And I think you ought to go. Is that coat paid for, Gilbert?

GILBERT. Not yet, beloved.

MAUDE. (*To Janie.*) Take it off.

ARNOLD. (*Hastily.*) No!

MAUDE. You keep quiet. You've done enough damage already. Not content with ruining Miss Tipdale, you're now flaunting your infidelities under her very nose. (*To Janie.*) Take it off.

JANIE. I can't.

MAUDE. Take it off.

JANIE. I can't!

MAUDE. Why not?

JANIE. Because I usually do this sort of thing to music. (*Janie, her back to audience, opens the coat. And, without the men seeing,*

46

gives Maude a very quick glimpse. Janie breaks away and wraps the coat around her. Maude slowly sits on the settee, just gaping out front. Gilbert walks slowly across with a glass and champagne bottle. He puts the glass in Maude's hand and fills it with champagne. Maude does not react but stays transfixed.)
GILBERT. Or would you rather have a brandy?

THE CURTAIN FALLS

ACT TWO

The action is continuous.

MAUDE. (*Gives Janie a glance.*) Gilbert, I'm overwhelmed!

GILBERT. I know exactly what you mean, darling.

MAUDE. Where are your clothes, girl?

JANIE. Mr. Crouch threw them out of the window.

MAUDE. (*Amazed.*) Out of the—? Is this true, Arnold?

ARNOLD. That part of it is true, yes, but—

GILBERT. You keep quiet till you're asked the other part.

MAUDE. Arnold, I will make no comment on this sinister fetish of yours but, if only to preserve the good name of the firm, I think you should have retrieved the young lady's clothes.

ARNOLD. I couldn't. They landed on top of a bus and went to Westminster Abbey!

MAUDE. Why didn't you get some more?

JANIE. He did.

MAUDE. (*To Arnold.*) I suppose you felt compelled to throw those out of the window as well?

ARNOLD. (*Almost in tears.*) Yes.

GILBERT. Don't keep on, Maude. Have pity on the wretch.

MAUDE. I will leave you, Mr. Crouch, to resolve your intrigue as best you can—but you should thank heaven in your prayers that you have such a staunch friend as my Gilbert. (*As Maude kisses him, Gilbert smiles and "chalks" another one up to himself. Maude goes up c. steps and meets Miss Tipdale who enters from door u. L. Miss Tipdale leaves door open. Overcome at the sight of Miss Tipdale.*) You poor, poor dear, you must be brave, be very brave. (*Gives her a mothering kiss, sighs deeply and exits.*)

GILBERT. (*To Miss Tipdale.*) Have you got Mrs. McMichael's underwear, Tippers?

MISS TIPDALE. Not yet, no.

GILBERT. What are you doing, knitting 'em?

MISS TIPDALE. I've been keeping a young lady engaged in conversation.

GILBERT. You haven't got time for that. What young lady?

48

MISS TIPDALE. (*Trying to be diplomatic.*) A Mrs. Lawson.

GILBERT. Mrs. Lawson?

MISS TIPDALE. Mrs. Sue Lawson.

GILBERT. We don't know her.

MISS TIPDALE. The lady who was here with—

GILBERT. We know her!

JANIE. (*To Gilbert.*) Not another of your—

GILBERT. Good heavens, no! (*To Arnold.*) She's nothing to do with me, is she?

ARNOLD. Don't you talk to me.

GILBERT. (*To Janie.*) Don't you talk to him.

JANIE. I don't want to talk to anyone, I just want some clothes.

MISS TIPDALE. I quite agree with you, madam.

JANIE. Then I can slip into my *two* fur coats and go for a spin in my lovely new sports car, eh, Gillie?

GILBERT. (*Concerned.*) Janie, my dear, my darling, er— (*To Miss Tipdale.*) That'll be all, Tippers, thank you.

MISS TIPDALE. What about Mrs. Lawson?

GILBERT. What does the silly girl want?

MISS TIPDALE. It's about that Canadian mink. She says she think it's beginning to look frightened already.

GILBERT. Ssh!

MISS TIPDALE. She's brought it back and wants to change—

GILBERT. Brought it back? What a stroke of luck. D'you know it's my first today?

JANIE. What Canadian mink is this, Gillie?

GILBERT. It's yours, my darling, it's just come back from the cleaners. It hasn't shrunk, has it?

MISS TIPDALE. (*Puzzled.*) I don't think so.

GILBERT. I don't trust these washing machines! Show the coat in, and the girl out, Miss Tipdale. (*Bundles Miss Tipdale out.*) All is now sweetness and light! (*He kisses Janie and then he turns to Arnold with arms outstretched.*)

ARNOLD. Don't you dare, Mr. Bodley.

GILBERT. Oh, don't be such a wet blanket. You can have Tippers. Janie can have her mink and I can have fun.

JANIE. Ah yes, but first my underclothes.

GILBERT. Yes—well, Tippers can go for them any time now.

JANIE. (*Has a bright idea.*) Wait a minute, you've got my overnight bag at your flat.

GILBERT. Of course, I'll send Tippers round there immediately.

ARNOLD. (*Triumphantly.*) If Mrs. Bodley hasn't got there first.

GILBERT. (*Aghast.*) Ah!

ARNOLD. (*Delighted.*) Ah! (*Arnold wipes clean the imaginary slate and chalks up one for himself.*) Now, Mr. Bodley, the ball's in your court.

GILBERT. Arnold, hold the fort till I get back.

ARNOLD. Why should I lift a finger for you?

GILBERT. Arnold! If our friendship has meant anything to you, stand by me now.

ARNOLD. I haven't noticed much friendship so far today.

GILBERT. See me through this, Arnold, and I promise never to leave the straight and narrow again.

ARNOLD. On your honour?

GILBERT. On my honour. (*Bravely to Janie.*) I've learnt my lesson. From this time forth I shall be faithful to Maude.

ARNOLD. Very well, then. You can count on my support. But remember—"Be thou faithful unto death."

GILBERT. Oh, you're so right. (*He pinches Janie's bottom, unseen by Arnold, and exits door* U. L., *having chalked one up, by door, unseen by the other two and leaving door open.*)

ARNOLD. Mrs. McMichael, that was a terrible thing you did to me.

JANIE. What was that, Arnie?

ARNOLD. Besmirching my character like that in front of Mrs. Bodley.

JANIE. D'you mean to say you'd be ashamed to have me as your lover?

ARNOLD. That's not what I meant.

JANIE. Well, I should think not, considering I've sheltered you under this very coat.

ARNOLD. Yes, I know. I shall never be able to look you in the face again. (*There is an altercation at the door* U. L.)

SUE. (*Off.*) I'm not giving it back. ARNOLD. (*To Janie.*) Excuse me a second, please. . . .

SUE. (*Enters carrying the mink.*) I'm swapping it.

MISS TIPDALE. (*Off.*) Yes, but you'll have to wait.

SUE. Well, I've been doing that for the past ten minutes. (*Miss Tipdale follows her in, leaving door open.*)

MISS TIPDALE. Mr. Crouch, will you see this young lady in my office? (*Arnold hurries to them and shoos Sue back* L. *along rostrum. Miss Tipdale back to below door—urging Sue to go.*)

ARNOLD. (*Flustered.*) Yes, I think I'd better.

SUE. Well, I've got to be back in my office in five minutes.

ARNOLD. We'll bear it in mind. (*He takes her arm and is about to propel her through the door* U. L. *when Janie speaks.*)

JANIE. Miss!

SUE. Eh—yes?

JANIE. You can leave the coat.

SUE. I beg your pardon?

JANIE. I said leave the coat.

SUE. Not until Mr. Crouch says whether or not I can swap it for another one!

JANIE. Swap it? (*There is a fractional pause.*)

MISS TIPDALE. If you want me, I shall be outside.

ARNOLD. So will I. (*He turns to follow out Miss Tipdale but she whispers urgently that he must remain and sort out the situation. He whispers equally urgently that he is not up to it. The two girls, having given each other a cursory glance, are watching the inaudible but frantic discussion at the door. Arnold turns to see if they are watching. Miss Tipdale takes this opportunity to exit and when Arnold turns to follow he finds the door banged in his face. He smiles at the girls.*) Well, this is cosy, isn't it? Shall we see if we have a basis for discussion and discover what the score is? Do you two ladies know each other?

JANIE AND SUE. (*Slightly tense.*) No.

ARNOLD. (*To audience.*) Love—15. (*To Sue.*) I think you should know who this lady is.

JANIE. You don't have to introduce me to the girl from the cleaners.

SUE. What are you going on about? I'm nothing to do with the cleaners.

JANIE. Well, how did you get that coat?

SUE. Well, if you must know, my friend gave it to me.

ARNOLD. (*To audience.*) 15—all.

JANIE. Your friend?

ARNOLD. (*Quickly stepping in between.*) This is Mrs. McMichael!

SUE. Just because she looks all posh she thinks I'm not good enough to wear a fur coat.

ARNOLD. I'm sure that's not the case, is it, Mrs. McMichael?

SUE. (*Pressing on.*) Well, I bet I'm as good as she is underneath.

ARNOLD. Let's hope it won't be put to the test.

JANIE. What I don't see is how your friend bought my coat.

SUE. Well, he did and it's not your coat. And my friend is **very** influential—

ARNOLD. Please, let me do the introductions. This is Mrs. McMichael, Mrs. *Harry* McMichael, she's the wife of Mr. McMichael, Mr. Harry McMichael.

JANIE. I think we've gathered who I am by now.

ARNOLD. I wouldn't bank on it.

SUE. (*In open-mouthed astonishment.*) You're not Mrs. **Harry** McMichael?

ARNOLD. (*To audience.*) Advantage Crouch.

JANIE. You were going to tell me about your friend, who gave you that coat.

SUE. Was I? Oh, yes. (*Points to Arnold.*) It's him. (*Arnold closes his eyes at the inevitability of it all.*)

ARNOLD. (*To audience.*) New balls, please.

JANIE. (*To Arnold.*) You miserable little man.

ARNOLD. Yes, I am rather, aren't I? I suppose there would be no use denying it?

SUE. None at all.

ARNOLD. I thought not. (*Miss Tipdale hurries in from* U. L. *opening door, and down steps* L., *leaving door open.*)

MISS TIPDALE. Mr. Crouch! Mr. Crouch!

ARNOLD. What is it!? What is it!?

MISS TIPDALE. It's Mrs. Bodley.

ARNOLD. (*Without thinking.*) We're just good friends. I mean, what about her?

MISS TIPDALE. Mr. Bodley has just rung up from the flat.

ARNOLD. Oh, he got there. Good.

MISS TIPDALE. No, it's not good. The "you know whats" weren't laid out on the bed and neither was Mrs. Bodley.

ARNOLD. Oh, dear. Is she coming back here?

MISS TIPDALE. Presumably, yes. So for goodness' sake get rid of "you know who." (*She indicates Janie.*)

ARNOLD. How can I without her "you know whats"?

SUE. Is this a private game or can anyone join in?

ARNOLD. (*To Sue.*) It's private! (*To Miss Tipdale.*) Go downstairs and give me a ring the minute you see Mrs. Bodley coming.

MISS TIPDALE. Yes, but what about the "you know whats"?

ARNOLD. Forget them. I've got an idea, go on.

MISS TIPDALE. Mr. Crouch, I'm not sure that—

ARNOLD. Do as you're told, Ambrosine!

MISS TIPDALE. (*Overcome.*) Oh, Arnold. (*She exits in a trance, leaving Arnold gazing after her tenderly.*)

JANIE. (*To Arnold.*) Well, that wasn't very clever. She was meant to be getting me some clothes.

SUE. What's going on here?

ARNOLD. Nothing untoward. It's just that Mrs. McMichael hasn't got any clothes on.

SUE. No clothes on?

JANIE. No.

SUE. (*To Arnold, referring to Janie.*) Funny lady. (*Arnold reacts to this.*)

ARNOLD. The point is she has got to have a dress and get out of here immediately, so the sooner you oblige the better.

JANIE. Marvellous!

SUE. Certainly not. I don't owe her any favours.

ARNOLD. I suggest you think again. She's been extremely generous. Consider what you've had that is rightly hers.

JANIE. What's that?

ARNOLD. The coat, of course. What else?

SUE. Here, now wait a minute—

ARNOLD. No—at a time like this you must remember the old saying, "Do unto others as you yourself have been done— (*Then very quickly.*) BY!"

SUE. Where shall I change?

ARNOLD. Good girl, in here. (*Arnold opens storeroom door. Sue moves and then stops.*)

SUE. Hang on a second. If she's wearing my dress what am I going to wear?

ARNOLD. That's a very intelligent question.

SUE. Yes, and what's the answer?

ARNOLD. It's so simple it'll amaze you— (*He bundles her off and shuts the door.*) —and me.

JANIE. Well done! You're a bit of a dark horse, aren't you, Arnie?

ARNOLD. I—er—wouldn't say so, no.

JANIE. (*Advancing on him. Curiously.*) I must have a closer look at you.

ARNOLD. That won't be necessary.

JANIE. I wouldn't have let you under my coat if I'd known you were such a devil.

ARNOLD. Please! That was done in the heat of the moment.

JANIE. And you're not off the boil yet, are you? (*She straightens his tie.*)

ARNOLD. Please, Mrs. McMichael. (*She giggles and starts to tickle his neck.*) Please, Mrs. McMichael, please. (*Mrs. Frencham enters from the door* U. L. *Arnold has his back to her.*) Please, madam, please. (*Mrs. Frencham has walked down to Arnold's left.*)

MRS. FRENCHAM. Mr. Crouch!

ARNOLD. Ah!! (*He turns to see Mrs. Frencham.*) Oh—do forgive me. She was just tightening my straight . . . Yes . . . (*To Mrs. Frencham.*) Now, correct me if I'm wrong. You're Mrs. Frencham.

MRS. FRENCHAM. (*Slightly bemused.*) Well, of course.

ARNOLD. Are you sure?

MRS. FRENCHAM. Yes.

ARNOLD. I'm just checking. You're Mrs. Frencham and you're probably wondering who this lady is.

MRS. FRENCHAM. Not really.

ARNOLD. Very well, I'll tell you. (*To Janie.*) Can you think of any just cause or impediment why you two should not be joined in an introduction?

JANIE. Not offhand, no.

ARNOLD. Splendid. This is Mrs. Smith.

MRS. FRENCHAM. Oh, you're a new girl, are you?

JANIE. Well, yes, you could put it that way. How are you?

MRS. FRENCHAM. Not very well, thank you. It's been a morning. Have you ever been to the Chelsea Police Station?

JANIE. No.

MRS. FRENCHAM. Well, don't.

ARNOLD. Oh, yes, your car was towed away, wasn't it?

MRS. FRENCHAM. It's worse than that! When we went to collect it, Mr. Frencham got so angry he hit the policeman!

ARNOLD. Oh dear, no serious damage, I hope!

MRS. FRENCHAM. A very nasty bruise—right across the knuckles. I must get back there. So—I'll take my coat now. (*She indicates her coat which Janie is wearing.*)

ARNOLD. (*To audience.*) Game set and match.

54

JANIE. Your coat? (*Door* D. R. *opens and Sue appears in bra and panties. She is holding her dress.*)

SUE. My dress. (*She hesitates on seeing Mrs. Frencham. Brightly.*) Oh, sorry, wrong room. (*She exits, and shuts door. Mrs. Frencham looks at Arnold who shrugs.*)

MRS. FRENCHAM. If I could have my coat, please.

ARNOLD. Yes, madam! (*Arnold crosses to Janie and he takes her across to the cocktail cabinet at* D. L., *Janie hanging back.*) Slip it off in there, please.

JANIE. (*Sotto voice.*) But I've got nothing on under—

ARNOLD. That's not Mrs. Frencham's problem. She's desperate for that coat.

JANIE. Well, so am I.

ARNOLD. I'll find you something else. Now get in there before I smack your wrist. (*He pushes. her in and closes the door.*) I'm terribly sorry, staff is such a problem, these days, isn't it?

MRS. FRENCHAM. But isn't that your cocktail cabinet?

ARNOLD. (*Calmly.*) Yes, it is. (*The cocktail cabinet door opens. Janie's bare arm appears with the ocelot. Arnold takes it.*) Thank you. (*He closes the cabinet door.*)

MRS. FRENCHAM. (*Nodding towards cabinet.*) What about the —er—young lady?

ARNOLD. Don't worry about her. It's her lunch-break, anyway. Thank you for calling, Mrs. Frencham. (*Arnold pushes ocelot into Mrs. Frencham's shopping bag. Mrs. Frencham exits* U. L., *leaving door open. Miss Tipdale enters from* U. L., *leaving door open.*)

MISS TIPDALE. Mr. Crouch, Mr. Crouch . . . (*The exterior phone rings. Arnold lifts receiver and sits chair* R. *of table.*)

ARNOLD. Just a minute, Miss Tipdale. (*On phone.*) Hello— Bodley, Bodley and Crouch. Chelsea Police Station? Yes, yes, we know a Mr. Frencham. I understand he hit a policeman. . . . Oh, dear! He's hit the sergeant now. His wife's on her way over. . . . Oh, you've let him go! On his way here? Right. Goodbye! (*He puts phone down.*) Miss Tipdale, go and keep an eye out for Mrs. Bodley. And when Mr. Frencham arrives, sit on him. He is your responsibility.

MISS TIPDALE. Certainly, but in the meantime Mr. Lawson has arrived and he's yours.

ARNOLD. Mr. Lawson?

MISS TIPDALE. Husband of Mrs.

ARNOLD. No! I don't believe it.

MISS TIPDALE. Yes, and he is under the impression that his wife is here.

ARNOLD. Well, surely you adopted some form of modus operandi?

MISS TIPDALE. Modus operandi?

ARNOLD. Yes, you know, told him a thundering great lie.

MISS TIPDALE. Oh, yes, I said that, to the best of my knowledge, she left—

ARNOLD. Good girl. That's fine.

MISS TIPDALE. —And to allay his suspicions even further I said that you would be only too delighted to explain why she was here in the first place.

ARNOLD. Ooo! Miss Tipdale, if there is one person in the world who isn't qualified to deal with this sort of situation it's—

LAWSON. (*Entering from door* U. L.—*leaving it open.*) Mr. Crouch?

ARNOLD. Yes? (*Mr. Lawson comes into the room. He is a good-looking, tough young man.*)

LAWSON. Could I have a quick word with you, please?

MISS TIPDALE. If you want me I'll be at my post—desk. (*She exits* U. L., *leaving door open.*)

LAWSON. I think you might be able to help me.

ARNOLD. I doubt it.

LAWSON. I don't know what's going on around here but they told me at my wife's office that she was round here seeing her boss at a place called Bodley, Bodley and Crouch.

ARNOLD. Oh, yes, that's right, Mr. Bodley lunching, Mrs. Bodley walking and I'm crouching—I mean I'm Crouch.

LAWSON. Well, is she here?

ARNOLD. No. She's probably gone back to her office.

LAWSON. No, I've just come from there and they said she was here!

ARNOLD. Just a second. You're not Mr. Lawson, are you?

LAWSON. Yes. Who did you think I was?

ARNOLD. Do you know, I could have sworn my secretary said Kowalski?

LAWSON. That's nothing like Lawson, is it?

ARNOLD. No—no—I realise the mistake now I see you, Mr. Lawson.

LAWSON. Look—do you know where she is, please?

ARNOLD. Yes, she's having a cup of tea at the milk bar . . .

LAWSON. Milk bar!

ARNOLD. . . . Round the corner.

LAWSON. Why didn't you say so in the first place?

ARNOLD. Because I thought you were looking for Mrs. Kowalski.

LAWSON. Well, if she's not there, I'm coming back. (*He exits* u. l., *leaving door open.*)

ARNOLD. Very well, sir, thank you for calling. (*Janie enters from cocktail cabinet* d. l. *She is wearing the two tea towels, one draped around her bust and the other round her waist. They cover the essentials quite well. She stands in doorway,* d. l.)

JANIE. Arnie—!

ARNOLD. Mrs. McMichael. Are you sure they're safe?

JANIE. Depends what time you wash up.

LAWSON. (*Re-entering.*) Hey, what's the name of this milk bar? (*Janie "freezes" like a dummy. Arnold quickly takes out his handkerchief and flicks imaginary dust off her. Lawson watches bemused.*)

ARNOLD. Ah! I'm terribly sorry, can I help you?

LAWSON. What's the name of this milk bar, please?

ARNOLD. The—er—"Poor Cow."

LAWSON. Thank you. (*He exits* u. l., *leaving door open as Miss Tipdale enters,* u. l., *leaving door open. Janie relaxes her position.*)

MISS TIPDALE. Mr. Crouch, Mr. Crouch.

ARNOLD. Is it Mrs. Bodley?

MISS TIPDALE. No—Mr. McMichael.

ARNOLD. Oh, this is catastrophic! I've got two now. Mrs. McMichael here and Mrs. Lawson in there.

JANIE. Why should Harry be interested in your girl friend?

ARNOLD. No trick questions, please.

MISS TIPDALE. He's on his way up to the salon now. So Mrs. Lawson had better move over.

ARNOLD. Yes, yes, yes. . . . (*Stopping.*) No, no, no. I refuse to put all my bags in one exit. (*To Janie.*) Now get back in there. (*Very agitated, he opens wider the cocktail cabinet door* d. l. *and pushes Janie inside and shuts door. The storeroom door* r. *opens as the other closes and Sue comes out, still carrying her dress. She hands the dress to an amazed Miss Tipdale.*)

SUE. My dress. (*Sue exits storeroom and shuts door. Arnold goes to Miss Tipdale.*)

ARNOLD. That is for me. (*Miss Tipdale reacts to this strange remark. He takes the dress and moves to the cocktail room D. L. as Harry enters through door U. L. and meets Arnold at C. Arnold puts dress behind his back, backs to the window, and throws it out. He returns to Harry and shakes his hand overenthusiastically.*) God, it's good to see you, sir!

HARRY. Have you seen any more of my secretary?

ARNOLD. Yes, quite a—no, very little.

HARRY. She came back here to change the damn coat.

ARNOLD. No, she hasn't been here since she was here the last time before she went.

HARRY. I think you've got a screw loose or something.

ARNOLD. (*To Miss Tipdale.*) Make a note of that, will—

HARRY. (*Angrily.*) Don't start that again!

ARNOLD. (*Angrily.*) Don't start that again, Miss Tipdale!

HARRY. Listen, Mr.—er—

ARNOLD. Crouch, Arnold. Tipdale, Ambrosine.

HARRY. Will you shut up a minute?

ARNOLD. Certainly. (*The intercom telephone rings and Arnold lifts the receiver. To Harry.*) Excuse me. Hullo, Bodley, Bodley and Crouch. Oh, hullo, Phillips. (*He glances towards the window, looking worried.*) Yes, that's right. I threw it away. . . . Yes, it was one of my mother's. Did it get the bus all right? What . . . ? Hanging from the—? It's hanging from the— (*Looking at Miss Tipdale.*) Well, do your best to ignore it and we'll have a roundup at closing time. (*He puts the phone down and smiles at Harry.*)

HARRY. If I could have your undivided attention.

ARNOLD. Of course.

HARRY. About twenty minutes ago Mrs. Lawson left me.

ARNOLD. I'm very sorry to hear that.

HARRY. (*Ignoring this and moving to window.*) We were having a drink in that pub over the road. (*Arnold suddenly notices that the mink is on the settee.*)

ARNOLD. The mink!

HARRY. No. "The Red Lion," I think.

ARNOLD. Oh, the Red Lion. . . . (*Harry looks out of the window to check on the name of the pub. Arnold quickly rolls the mink up in the rug which is in front of the settee.*)

HARRY. Yes, it is. (*He turns to Arnold.*) "The Red Lion," I can see from here. Anyway, we were having . . . (*Harry stops on seeing Arnold standing there with a rolled-up rug. Arnold immediately heads for the balcony, shakes the fur coat out of the carpet and into the street.)*

ARNOLD. That's better, isn't it? *(Putting the rug back.)* Much better after that little shake. It gets very grubby down here. I just wish people wouldn't walk on it, that's all. Now, where were we?

HARRY. *(Controlling himself.)* I was saying that I've been waiting for my secretary.

ARNOLD. Oh, yes.

HARRY. So where is she?

ARNOLD. Definitely not here.

HARRY. Does that mean that she's been and gone or that she never even arrived?

ARNOLD. Yes.

HARRY. Yes, what?

ARNOLD. Yes, "please."

MISS TIPDALE. *(Still agitated about the coat.)* Oh, Mr. Crouch, I'll just pop downstairs and get the— *(She waves towards the window.)*

HARRY. *(Firmly.)* You stay where you are. *(The intercom telephone rings.)*

ARNOLD. Excuse me. *(On phone.)* Bodley, Bodley and Crouch. Mr. Bodley out on a job, Mrs. Bodley out on a job and I'm Crouch—out on a limb. Hullo, Phillips . . . Something else from our—er— Yes, we know all about it. . . . *(Airily.)* Well, it hadn't been out for a walk today so—er . . . No. We don't want it back up here . . . keep it in the office, give it a dog biscuit and a saucer of milk. *(He puts phone down and smiles at Harry. Harry glares at him and then turns to Miss Tipdale, coming to L. of her.)*

HARRY. *(To Miss Tipdale.)* Look, have you seen my secretary?

ARNOLD. No. *(Harry glares at him.)*

HARRY. *(To Miss Tipdale.)* Well, have you?

MISS TIPDALE. Not since she was here the last time before she went.

HARRY. Oh, God! *(He smacks his forehead and walks up C. steps towards the window. As he turns his back Sue comes out of the storeroom and is about to say "it's cold" when she sees Harry and stops dead. Arnold dashes over, pushes her back into the storeroom and slams the door. Harry, at C. on rostrum, turns at the noise to*

59

see Arnold fiddling with the lock. Sarcastically:) Oh, it's locked. It's quite definitely locked.

MISS TIPDALE. Yes, I'll make a note of that, Mr. McMichael.

HARRY. No, look, I think I'd rather see this partner of yours, Bodley.

MISS TIPDALE. He's out!

ARNOLD. Yes. He's gone to bed for a bit. (*Arnold realises what he has said.*)

HARRY. Why? Is he sick?

ARNOLD. No, no, he's as fit as a fiddle. It's just that his wife wanted to see him rather urgently.

HARRY. What, in bed?

ARNOLD. Yes, well, she's been away for two weeks.

HARRY. (*Sexily.*) They must be rather eager.

ARNOLD. Oh, they are, yes. (*Gilbert staggers into the room and leans against the door, breathless. He pours himself a glass of champagne without noticing the assembled company. Harry looks from Gilbert to Arnold and back again to Gilbert with something approaching admiration.*)

MISS TIPDALE. Are you all right, Mr. Bodley?

GILBERT. I haven't stopped since I left. (*Harry, quite impressed, looks at Arnold again.*)

ARNOLD. We have a visitor, Mr. Bodley.

GILBERT. (*Ignoring this.*) Has Maude shown up here?

ARNOLD. No.

GILBERT. Get outside, Tippers! Give me a buzz the moment she storms in.

MISS TIPDALE. Very good, Mr. Bodley. (*Miss Tipdale exits door U. L., leaving it open. Gilbert sits chair L. of table.*)

ARNOLD. Mr. Bodley, we have a visitor!

GILBERT. I don't care! At the moment I'm only interested in (*Sees him.*) Mr. McMichael!

HARRY. Nice to meet somebody else who believes in mixing a lot of pleasure with his business.

GILBERT. (*Worried.*) Pleasure?

HARRY. Yes, you and your wife.

GILBERT. My wife! She won't be satisfied till she has me swinging from the chandelier. (*Harry laughs and nudges Arnold. They both look at chandelier. Gilbert can't understand and looks at Arnold, then at chandelier.*)

ARNOLD. Mr. McMichael returned because he was under the erroneous impression that his secretary was here.

GILBERT. Ah. Is she?

ARNOLD. (*Nodding.*) No, she isn't.

GILBERT. (*Not understanding.*) What?

ARNOLD. No, she isn't *here*. She's— (*Arnold points surreptitiously to the storeroom and tries to mime that Sue is now in there, wearing only a bra and panties.*)

GILBERT. (*To Harry.*) She isn't here!

HARRY. No, you see I just don't understand what's been happening since I was here last.

GILBERT. To be perfectly honest, neither do I.

ARNOLD. (*To Gilbert.*) Apparently Mrs. Lawson said she was coming back to exchange the mink.

GILBERT. (*Cheerfully.*) Well, very likely she exchanged it and went.

HARRY. No, no. That's what I suggested, but your colleague said she definitely didn't return.

GILBERT. (*To Arnold.*) Why the hell did you say that?

ARNOLD. (*Angrily.*) Why the hell do I say anything? (*Again he points to door D. R. and tries the mime again.*)

GILBERT. (*To Harry.*) You must forgive Mr. Crouch. He's been labouring under a severe handicap for some time.

HARRY. Oh really, what's that?

GILBERT. His brain— (*Opening the door R. a little.*) He's been known to have sudden fits of (*Sees Sue.*) madness! (*He bangs the door shut.*)

HARRY. (*Inadvertently shouting in Arnold's ear.*) Don't do that!

ARNOLD. (*Jumping.*) Don't do that!

HARRY. What's the matter with everyone?

GILBERT. Nothing. Nothing at all. I need a drink. (*Strides over to the cocktail cabinet.*)

ARNOLD. No!!! (*Gilbert reacts in bewilderment.*) You don't drink. You're teetotal.

GILBERT. Since when?

ARNOLD. Since you signed the pledge.

HARRY. But he was having a drink not long ago. ·

ARNOLD. That doesn't count. It was out of a glass.

GILBERT. I haven't signed any pledge. (*Opens the door, sees Janie,*

61

bangs it shut, puts his hands in his pockets and smiles.) Anyone for hot chocolate?

HARRY. (*Patience finally gone.*) Would you two like to know something?

ARNOLD. (*Swallowing.*) Yes, please.

HARRY. I think you're both mad.

GILBERT. Oh, we are, we are. (*To Arnold.*) Aren't we?

ARNOLD. Yes, we are, we are. It's working with fur. It's mink-omania—it softens the tissues.

HARRY. There'll be more than tissues get softened unless I get satisfaction. Has Mrs. Lawson been here?

GILBERT. We—we—I—I—she   ARNOLD. She—she—we—we
—she—who?   —I—I—who?

HARRY. I just want yes or no.

GILBERT. (*To Arnold.*) Which d'you fancy?

HARRY. *Has she been here?*

GILBERT. Well, of course she was here. But I'm almost positive she left with you.

HARRY. I know she did, but that was half an hour ago. We only went up the street to that pub and she suddenly decided to change the coat. (*He goes up to the balcony.*) She left the pub and came back here. (*Points out the window.*) It's only a hundred yards, and she's been gone— (*He stops and his attention is arrested by something below.*) Excuse me, I won't be long. (*He walks quickly to the door.*)

GILBERT. (*Hopefully.*) Seen her?

HARRY. No, I'm just going down to inspect your flagpole.

ARNOLD. Why?

HARRY. I think you're flying Mrs. Lawson's colours. (*Exits and shuts door* U. L.)

GILBERT. (*Rushes to see.*) That's her dress! (*He looks.*) You've done it again!

ARNOLD. If only you knew what I've been through since you left.

GILBERT. I can imagine.

ARNOLD. I've done my best, Bodley.

GILBERT. Best! You've surpassed yourself. I leave you with one scantily clad female, I come back and find the place stuffed with 'em.

ARNOLD. Don't exaggerate.

GILBERT. What are you doing, starting a collection? Didn't you get my phone message about Maude?

ARNOLD. Of course I did.

GILBERT. Then why didn't you get Janie out of the way?

ARNOLD. I was trying to. I'd already got Mrs. Lawson's dress off—

GILBERT. So I've noticed. How did you manage it?

ARNOLD. I threatened to expose her.

GILBERT. You seem to have done a very good job. It's just as well you've managed to keep Harry's wife and his mistress apart or the balloon would have gone up.

ARNOLD. Well, as a matter of fact I haven't, but it didn't.

GILBERT. Explain yourself.

ARNOLD. The inevitable occurred.

GILBERT. D'you mean— (*Points to both doors.*) —they came face to face?

ARNOLD. Yes.

GILBERT. (*Amazed.*) And you averted disaster?

ARNOLD. (*Pleased with himself.*) Well—er—yes, I think I did.

GILBERT. But how?

ARNOLD. (*Nonchalantly.*) Well, I—er—passed Mrs. Lawson off as my—er—acquaintance.

GILBERT. Acquaintance?

ARNOLD. Well—as we fellows say, my— (*He whispers in Gilbert's ear. Gilbert reacts.*)

GILBERT. Well done, Crouch. (*Shakes Arnold's hand.*)

ARNOLD. Well, I did say I'd hold the fort.

GILBERT. I must say, you've come on a treat. You begin the day as an old stick-in-the-mud and before lunch even you've bagged yourself a brace of mistresses and half a lady's wardrobe.

ARNOLD. (*Rubbing his hands with glee.*) I know. I love it. (*Suddenly remembering.*) There is something I forgot to mention.

GILBERT. Surprise me.

ARNOLD. Mr. Lawson turned up.

GILBERT. Lawson?

ARNOLD. The husband of Mrs.

GILBERT. No! What did you do?

ARNOLD. Well, it was a bit of a problem. So I sent him to the Poor Cow.

GILBERT. The Poor Cow?

ARNOLD. The milk bar round the corner. (*He picks up phone.*)

GILBERT. Congratulations— (*Then stops.*) There isn't a milk bar round the corner.

ARNOLD. I know. That's the problem. (*On phone.*) Send up Miss Tipdale. (*He puts phone down.*) Now look, before everybody gets back these two young ladies must be re-clothed and removed.

GILBERT. But how, Crouch, how?

ARNOLD. I suggest for a start we forget the proprieties.

GILBERT. Certainly— What proprieties?

ARNOLD. Little things like underclothes and dresses. Why don't we give them two of our longest and warmest beavers, hail two taxis and then bid them farewell?

GILBERT. (*To audience.*) So simple, too. (*Miss Tipdale enters from door* U. L. *and leaves it open.*)

MISS TIPDALE. Mr. Bodley, I've been sent up.

GILBERT. It happens to us all.

ARNOLD. Miss Tipdale, go and see Mrs. Rowe. I want two beavers immediately.

GILBERT. The longest.

ARNOLD. And the cheapest. Hurry up and don't dilly-dally on the way.

MISS TIPDALE. Mr. Crouch.

ARNOLD. Yes?

MISS TIPDALE. May I say something?

ARNOLD. (*Looking at watch.*) Yes, but not very much.

MISS TIPDALE. (*With admiration.*) The way you've behaved to-day has been magnificent to behold.

ARNOLD. Oh, thank you, Miss Tipdale.

MISS TIPDALE. In fact, you've touched me here. (*She puts her hand to her bosom and then exits door* U. L. *and closes it.*)

GILBERT. You *have* made progress, haven't you?

ARNOLD. She was being metaphoric.

GILBERT. Yes. And who were you being?

ARNOLD. She simply realizes the lengths I've gone to, to save your miserable skin.

GILBERT. (*To audience.*) Cocky with it now.

ARNOLD. I'm going to get the beavers. You stand guard in case Lawson comes back.

GILBERT. Comes back?

ARNOLD. Yes, from the Poor Cow.

GILBERT. Oh, Lord. (*Looking at door* D. R.)

ARNOLD. And if Mr. McMichael returns with Mrs. Lawson's dress, plead ignorance.

GILBERT. (*Worried.*) Ignorance. Right.

ARNOLD. And if Mrs. Bodley gets back before I do—

GILBERT. Yes?

ARNOLD. God help you. (*He exits* U. L., *leaving door open, as Janie enters from cocktail cabinet. She stays in doorway, with one hand on the door.*)

JANIE. Has Harry gone?

GILBERT. Yes, and you're leaving immediately.

JANIE. In these? (*She indicates the tea towels.*)

GILBERT. Don't worry, we're going to get you a beaver down to your ankles.

JANIE. As well as my mink?

GILBERT. Yes, yes, yes.

JANIE. And my car?

GILBERT. Yes, yes, yes. Now stay there until I say it's all clear. (*Sue appears in doorway* D. R., *keeping hand on door.*)

SUE. Mr. Bodley! If I stay in here much longer, all my assets will be frozen.

GILBERT. Don't worry, we're giving you a beautiful beaver in place of that rotten old dyed rabbit.

SUE. When?

GILBERT. When I say it's all clear. Now stay there until you come under starter's orders.

JANIE. (*Calling across to Sue good-naturedly.*) See you at the starting gate, sweetie. (*Both the doors are closed.*)

GILBERT. (*To audience.*) If I play my cards right, I may get the autumn double up. (*Mr. Frencham enters from* U. L., *leaving door open. He looks a bit upset.*)

MR. FRENCHAM. Oh. I'm looking for Crouch.

GILBERT. I'm afraid he's unavailable at the moment, sir. Who shall I say called?

MR. FRENCHAM. Who are you?

GILBERT. Gilbert Bodley, sir. I don't think we've . . .

MR. FRENCHAM. (*Coming down* C. *steps.*) No, no, we haven't. I've had one hell of a time. Pushed from pillar to post.

GILBERT. I'm sorry to hear that, sir.

MR. FRENCHAM. So, tell her I'm here, will you?

GILBERT. Who?

MR. FRENCHAM. My wife, of course.

GILBERT. Your wife?

MR. FRENCHAM. Yes. You got my message, didn't you? Well, I've come back for her. . . .

GILBERT. (*Suddenly realising that this must be Mr. Lawson.*) Oh . . . you've come back for your wife.

MR. FRENCHAM. Yes. You wouldn't believe the trouble I've had trying to . . .

GILBERT. Ah, I suppose you've been wondering why you couldn't find the "Poor Cow."

MR. FRENCHAM. I beg your pardon?

GILBERT. I can explain the entire situation for you, sir.

MR. FRENCHAM. Good.

GILBERT. There isn't one.

MR. FRENCHAM. (*Bemused.*) Oh— Look— Did you give my wife that blasted coat?

GILBERT. (*Quickly.*) No! No! Not me! I am responsible for many things. But you can't lay your wife at my door.

MR. FRENCHAM. (*Desperately trying to follow.*) Eh?

GILBERT. I met your wife for the first time today and the only thought that passed through my mind was that a sweet little thing she was.

MR. FRENCHAM. (*Frowning.*) My wife?

GILBERT. She's a little poppet.

MR. FRENCHAM. (*Getting impatient.*) Look, I've just spent a very trying half hour with the police—

GILBERT. The police?!

MR. FRENCHAM. Yes.

GILBERT. But it's not as serious as all that, surely, sir?

MR. FRENCHAM. They seemed to think it was. Going to be a court case, you know.

GILBERT. No— No— I'll tell you everything. Everything!

MR. FRENCHAM. Dammit, all I want to know is where my wife's got to.

GILBERT. All right, but the fact that she's been running around here in bra and pants is nothing to do with me.

MR. FRENCHAM. Bra and pants?

GILBERT. Yes, you see it was Crouch's idea to get her dress off, not mine.

MR. FRENCHAM. (*Astonished.*) Crouch took her dress off?

GILBERT. Yes, but he only wanted to borrow it.

MR. FRENCHAM. Crouch wanted to borrow my wife's dress?!

GILBERT. Yes.

MR. FRENCHAM. Look, Bodley—I think you'r better start at the beginning.

GILBERT. Well, sir, if you're going to involve the police, I feel it my duty to make it quite clear that Bodley, Bodley, and Crouch are completely innocent. You see, it all started with the coat.

MR. FRENCHAM. I know it started with the coat. But how did it finish with bra and pants?

GILBERT. (*Surprised.*) Oh—you know about the coat?

MR. FRENCHAM. Yes.

GILBERT. And Harry?

MR. FRENCHAM. Harry?

GILBERT. You don't know about Harry?

MR. FRENCHAM. No.

GILBERT. Harry, sir, has taken advantage of your wife.

MR. FRENCHAM. Ye gods!

GILBERT. This must come as a bit of a shock.

MR. FRENCHAM. It certainly does. I thought the old girl was past it.

GILBERT. Past it? (*Looks at the storeroom door.*) She's ripe for it.

MR. FRENCHAM. My wife—ripe?

GILBERT. Don't you think she is?

MR. FRENCHAM. It depends what you mean by ripe.

GILBERT. Like a peach. She must be fighting them off all the time. Pestered by every Tom, Dick—

MR. FRENCHAM. And Harry, yes. Do you mind if I sit down? Bit of a facer when the boot's on the other foot. Oh, I blame myself. You know what it's like when you're in the Navy.

GILBERT. Pretty good, I should imagine.

MR. FRENCHAM. Oh, I've never gone mad. Just the occasional fling. Too busy enjoying myself, I suppose, to appreciate the little woman back home.

GILBERT. It's a common failing, sir.

MR. FRENCHAM. If only one could recapture those halcyon honeymoon days.

GILBERT. (*Points to storeroom door.*) Be our guest, sir.

MR. FRENCHAM. I beg your pardon?

GILBERT. You want to recapture your lost youth, don't you?

MR. FRENCHAM. Oh, if only I could.

GILBERT. (*Opens door.*) Go in there, sir. Grab her and don't take no for an answer. (*Mr. Frencham pulls himself up to his full height and crosses to open door* D. R.)

MR. FRENCHAM. Hubba, hubba, hubba! (*He exits storeroom and Gilbert shuts door. Arnold hurries in from* U. L. *and shuts door.*)

ARNOLD. Mr. Bodley, stand by for action. Your wife's on her way up in the elevator.

GILBERT. God! I wonder how much she knows.

ARNOLD. You'll soon see.

GILBERT. As long as she never found those frilly things on the bed.

ARNOLD. The speed she's travelling, she found something.

GILBERT. Hell.

ARNOLD. Don't worry. It's our last remaining problem.

GILBERT. And the biggest. (*Sue opens the storeroom door firmly but politely. Mr. Frencham, looking very bewildered, comes out. Sue returns to the storeroom, shutting the door. Mr. Frencham crosses in silence to the door* U. L., *going up* C. *steps. He turns by the door.*)

MR. FRENCHAM. That's the most ridiculous conversation I've ever had. (*He exits* U. L., *leaving door open. Bodley and Arnold exchange a puzzled glance.*)

MAUDE. (*Off.*) Good afternoon, Mr. Frencham. Can't stay.

ARNOLD. (*Sotto voce.*) It's   GILBERT. (*Sotto voce.*) This
Mrs. Bodley.   is it.

(*Maude enters from* U. L., *leaving door open.*)

MAUDE. Gilbert!

GILBERT. (*Charged with emotion.*) Maude! Before you say anything, remember we've been married for twenty years.

MAUDE. And in all that time you've never done anything more sweet or loving.

GILBERT. I can explain it all— (*He realises what Maude has said and goes almost cross-eyed with confusion.*) Maude, don't play me like a damned fish. Reel me in and hit me on the head.

MAUDE. What do you mean, darling?

GILBERT. Whatever you've got to say, say it.

MAUDE. I've just said it.

GILBERT. Did you? I must have missed it.

ARNOLD. So did I. Would you mind going out and coming in again?

GILBERT. Whatever you have to do, Maude, can be done in front of our dear friend here. (*He indicates Arnold.*)

MAUDE. Oh, very well, if you say so. (*She kisses him warmly. Arnold stands there, not knowing what to do. Gilbert comes out of the embrace looking astonished. He looks blankly at Arnold.*)

GILBERT. What happened? (*By way of explanation Arnold gives Gilbert a quick kiss on the cheek. To Arnold.*) The shock must have turned her brain.

MAUDE. I must admit it was a bit of a surprise.

GILBERT. But you sound genuinely pleased.

MAUDE. Of course, I am, darling. And what is so flattering is—they're the right size. (*Gilbert and Arnold for a second are completely bemused.*)

GILBERT. (*Trying to keep pace.*) Are they?

MAUDE. Yes. But the way you'd laid them all out on the bed for me, it was like coming back to a love-nest. (*The truth begins to dawn on Gilbert, who beams with delight. Arnold is still attempting to work it all out.*)

GILBERT. (*To Maude.*) Just a silly little home-coming present.

ARNOLD. (*Thinking out loud.*) But you didn't know she was coming home. (*Gilbert nudges Arnold in the stomach with his elbow. Arnold is winded.*)

GILBERT. (*With false gaiety.*) What Arnold means is that I didn't know *exactly* when you were coming home, Maude. That's what you meant, Arnold, wasn't it? Arnold!

ARNOLD. (*Still slightly winded.*) I think it was, yes.

GILBERT. (*To Maude.*) I don't understand how I missed you at the flat. Where were you?

MAUDE. Oh, I was there all the time.

GILBERT. I didn't see you anywhere.

MAUDE. I was having a bath. To freshen up. To tell you the truth I wondered what had happened to you.

GILBERT. Why was that?

MAUDE. Well, I heard you rush in through the front door, go into the bedroom, scream and rush out again.

GILBERT. Oh, yes. I remember.

69

MAUDE. Why did you do that?

GILBERT. I beg your pardon?

ARNOLD. She said why did you do that? (*Gilbert nudges Arnold again, who sees it coming and jumps away.*)

GILBERT. I screamed, Maude, because you weren't there. I expected to find you and the frilly things on the bed and you'd both gone.

MAUDE. So it was a cry of anguish.

GILBERT. Indeed it was.

MAUDE. Silly boy. And as for my dear little overnight bag. (*She moves to door U. L. to get case.*)

GILBERT. (*With a horrified look to Arnold, sotto voce.*) Overnight bag?—Janie's . . . !!

MAUDE. (*Coming back with case.*) I'm mad about it. Oh, you really are so generous, darling. I tried to open it, but it seems to be locked.

GILBERT. (*To Arnold, sotto voce.*) Lucky me.

MAUDE. I beg your pardon?

GILBERT. No key.

MAUDE. Oh, what a pity. (*Weighing up case.*) If I know my Gilbert he's got some other treats in store for me.

GILBERT. You don't want them all at once, do you?

MAUDE. One of my keys may fit. (*She searches in her handbag. Gilbert turns and throws the case to Arnold who in turn throws it over the balcony. Arnold looks staggered for a moment, then goes to the desk, stands by the telephone and waits for it to ring. Meanwhile Maude has found a bunch of keys and looks round for the hold-all. Gilbert comes down to her and helpfully joins in the fruitless search. The telephone rings. Arnold picks it up automatically and without waiting to hear who is on the other end hands the receiver out to Gilbert.*)

ARNOLD. It's for you.

GILBERT. Oh, thank you. (*Into the phone.*) Bodley here— Oh, hello, Phillips— Really? (*Offhand.*) . . . There's no damage, is there? Just the top of your head. . . . What do you mean—danger money? No, no, there's no more to come. . . . (*To Arnold.*) You haven't got anything else, Arnold, have you?

ARNOLD. No, I've run out. You haven't anything, have you, Mrs.—?

GILBERT. (*Continuing.*) No, Arnold's run out! No, that's the

70

lot. . . . (*Shouting.*) I said, that's the lot. . . . Yes, it's all clear. . . . (*Shouting.*) I said, it's ALL CLEAR! (*Janie—in tea towels—from door* D. L. *and Sue—in bra and pants—from door* D. R. *take this as their cue to come out. Sue closes her door, Janie leaves hers open. They run to* U. S. C. *where they meet Miss Tipdale who has entered from door* U. L. *and come to* C. *on rostrum, carrying two full-length beaver coats. Janie and Sue each take one, and rush out of door* U. L. *Arnold, Gilbert and Maude stand there transfixed for a moment.*)

MAUDE. (*Finally.*) What's going on?

GILBERT. We've been robbed!!

ARNOLD. (*Falsely urgent.*) Go and get the coats, Miss Tipdale.

MISS TIPDALE. At once, Mr. Crouch. (*Miss Tipdale exits door* U. L., *leaving it open.*)

MAUDE. Wait a minute. One of those was your girl friend, Arnold.

ARNOLD. I do believe it was, yes.

MAUDE. (*Bemused.*) She came out of the cocktail cabinet.

ARNOLD. So she did.

MAUDE. How long had she been in there?

GILBERT. (*Looks at watch.*) Oh, ages. We ordered those drinks hours ago.

MAUDE. (*Not believing it.*) I see. And who's the other girl?

ARNOLD. That's the afternoon shift.

MAUDE. Arnold! (*She exits door* U. L., *leaving it open.*)

ARNOLD. (*Goes to the internal phone and dials two figures.*) I'll get the doorman and tell him to stand by for action— (*Into phone.*) Ah, is that you? Good. this is me again. There are two fast beavers coming down the stairs, let them out. . . . That's right. And Mrs. Bodley's coming down by elevator—shut her in. . . . Yes, that's it. Beavers out, Bodley in. (*Replaces receiver. Sue returns hurriedly through door* L., *heading into cocktail cabinet.*)

SUE. (*Speaking as she comes.*) Harry's on his way up and he's got my dress off the flagpole. (*Janie enters* U. L. *and rushes along rostrum and down steps* R. *She hands two tea towels to Arnold. Both girls are wearing beaver coats.*)

JANIE. (*Speaking as she comes.*) Look out. Harry's on his way up and— (*She stops and looks at Sue.*) What are you hiding for?

SUE. Me?

71

JANIE. Aren't you Arnold's girl friend?

SUE. What, still?

ARNOLD. Absolutely.

JANIE. Then why are you running away from my husband?

GILBERT. She's got a point there.

SUE. I don't know really, I get confused very easily.

ARNOLD. Why should she run away from your husband when she's got a perfectly good one of her own to run away from?

SUE. Yes, exactly, why—my husband?

ARNOLD. Certainly.

SUE. Charlie? He's not here, is he?

GILBERT. You bet he is—

ARNOLD. Young, short, slim.   GILBERT. Elderly, tall, plump. (*They look at each other in amazement.*)

SUE. What are you two going on about?

HARRY. (*Off.*) Bodley—Crouch?

GILBERT. (*To Janie.*) Later. (*Pushes her into storeroom.*)

ARNOLD. (*To Sue.*) Get in there. (*Pushing her into cocktail cabinet.*) Oh! Mrs. McMichael hasn't got her tea towels.

HARRY. (*Off.*) Bodley! (*Arnold drops tea towels on chair and hurries over to join Gilbert as Harry enters from U. L. with Sue's dress. He is furious. He leaves door open.*) What was Mrs. Lawson's dress doing on the flagpole?

ARNOLD. Waving?

HARRY. I demand an explanation.

GILBERT. (*To Arnold.*) How shall we play it?

ARNOLD. I think calmly, with just a hint of—er—

GILBERT. Hysteria?

ARNOLD. Yes, that's it.

HARRY. My secretary is walking about your place with no dress on and I want to know why.

ARNOLD. I don't think his curiosity is unwarranted, do you, Mr. Bodley?

GILBERT. Most reasonable. Mrs. Lawson in a state of 'deshabille," you say? I'm sure *one* of us would have noticed.

ARNOLD. I'll ask Miss Tipdale. She may have seen her trotting through the shop.

HARRY. What, with no dress on? She's up here somewhere.

GILBERT. On the balcony perhaps.

HARRY. Yes, or in this room here perhaps. (*He flings open store-*

72

*room door. Gilbert and Arnold freeze. Janie, who has obviously
had her ear to the keyhole, falls out and gets to* R. C. *Harry closes
the door without seeing her, turns to her, saying, "Now then—"
She turns and he is dumbfounded to see it is Janie.)* Now, then—
(After a moment.) This is my wife!

GILBERT. *(Politely.)* Pleased   ARNOLD. How do you do?
to meet you.

(The three of them shake hands.)

HARRY. *(Almost beside himself: to Janie.)* What the hell were
you doing in there?

JANIE. Choosing a coat. Do you like it ?

HARRY. Oh, don't give me that. Come on, we're going home. And
after that, I'm coming back here.

GILBERT. It's early closing today.

HARRY. You may be closing earlier than you think. And when
I do come back you're going to have to give me a thundering good
explanation.

GILBERT. Our man Crouch deals with all the complaints.

HARRY. *(To Janie.)* Right. Come on.

JANIE. Really, Harry. You are being tiresome.

HARRY. I've hardly started yet. I haven't made up my mind
whether to sue them or do them. Now then, take that coat off.

JANIE. What on earth for? *(Arnold and Gilbert are horrified.)*

HARRY. Because I don't want anything from this shop.

ARNOLD. No, we insist. It's the bargain of the month.

HARRY. I don't care. Take it off.

GILBERT. But she's paid for it.

HARRY. Take—it—off!

JANIE. Harry, precious, it's impossible.

HARRY. What do you mean it's impossible? When I say take it
off, I mean take it off. I'm still your husband, aren't I? I don't
know what you've been up to with these two characters here, but,
by George, when I get you home . . . *(Janie, screening herself
from the audience and Gilbert and Arnold, opens the coat for a
brief second to show Harry her state of undress. He stops dead in
his tracks as though pole-axed.)*

ARNOLD. *(Casually.)* I think it may rain.

GILBERT. I didn't hear the forecast.

ARNOLD. It wasn't very good for Hartford, Hereford, and Hamp-
shire.

HARRY. (*To himself in disbelief.*) My wife is stark naked. It's incredible.

ARNOLD. (*Aside to Gilbert.*) Mr. Bodley, he must have seen her like that before!

HARRY. (*Still dazed.*) Would you mind if I helped myself to a drink?

GILBERT. Certainly. (*Harry goes to cocktail cabinet D. L. as Arnold madly mimes to Gilbert that Sue is still in there. Gilbert looks unruffled.*)

HARRY. I'm going to drink a whole bottle of Scotch in one gulp.

JANIE. Now, Harry, you know you can't control your temper when you drink.

HARRY. I don't want to control my temper. I want to go berserk!

GILBERT. Now, naughty—naughty.

ARNOLD. Remember, least said soonest mended.

HARRY. I'm going to bust this place wide open. I'm going to stuff Crouch into a sheared raccoon and kick Bodley right up the ocelot. (*He flings open the cocktail cabinet door and Sue hands him a bottle of whiskey. He takes it without realising and half shuts the door.*) Oh, thank you. (*Then realises that Sue is there and opens door again; to Sue.*) What the hell are you doing in there?!

GILBERT. (*Getting his own back.*) Ah, so you two know each other?

HARRY. Know her?! (*Harry is about to explode but then realises that he can't say anything in front of Janie. Janie is looking slightly confused.*) No! (*To Sue.*) How do you do? My name's Harry McMichael.

SUE. How do you do, Mr. McMichael? I'm very pleased to meet you. I'm Sue Lawson.

HARRY. (*Awkwardly.*) Oh, really?

SUE. Well, I thought you'd like to know.

HARRY. Thank you. Yes. (*To Janie, airily.*) Darling, have you met Mrs. Lawson?

JANIE. Yes.

HARRY. Oh.

JANIE. She's Mr. Crouch's girl friend.

HARRY. (*Furious.*) Mr. Who's what?

ARNOLD. It was very sudden.

HARRY. I should think it was!

GILBERT. I'm sure you must feel very happy about it, though.

74

JANIE. Why should Harry be happy?

GILBERT. Well, if she's Mr. Crouch's girl friend, she can't be anybody else's anything else, can she?

ARNOLD. Ah. He's got a point there, Mrs. McMichael.

GILBERT. So how do you feel now about the situation?

HARRY. (*Innocently.*) What situation?

ARNOLD. Your wife having no clothes on.

HARRY. Ah, yes. (*Then realises and shrugs.*) Oh, well— That could happen to anybody, really.

GILBERT. Your husband is so understanding, Mrs. McMichael. (*Miss Tipdale enters from door* U. L., *leaving door open.*)

MISS TIPDALE. Look, I don't know who knows what, but I think you all ought to know that Mrs. Bodley is on her way up.

GILBERT. I thought we told the doorman to hold her in the elevator.

MISS TIPDALE. He did and she's fired him. (*Miss Tipdale exits door* U. L., *leaving door open.*)

ARNOLD. Back to your posts, everybody. Come on, quickly. . . . (*The girls automatically rush to their doors, Sue* D. L. *and Janie* R. *Harry starts to go with Sue.*) Mr. McMichael. Your wife went that way.

HARRY. Oh, yes, of course. (*He goes to door* R., *followed by Gilbert and Arnold, and then stops.*) Look— Pardon me a minute, but who the hell am I hiding from?

GILBERT. My wife!

HARRY. I've never even met your wife.

GILBERT. Let's keep it that way— I don't want to meet her either. All haste, Crouch! (*Gilbert and Arnold try to come in the door* D. R.)

HARRY. Not in here! My wife's got no clothes on. (*Gilbert and Arnold about-turn and head for the cocktail cabinet. They stop at* C.) Not with my secretary, either. (*Harry goes into storeroom and shuts door.*)

MAUDE. (*Off.*) Out of my way, Miss Tipdale.

MISS TIPDALE. (*Off.*) I can assure you—

MAUDE. (*Off.*) Out of my way! I'm going to kill both of them!!

ARNOLD. Bodley, it's curtains for us—

GILBERT. What a good idea. (*Gilbert and Arnold rush to the curtains and hide behind them, Gilbert* R.—*Arnold* L.)

MAUDE. (*Coming through door.*) They'll regret the day they

75

ever lied to me. (*Maude enters* U. L.) Gilbert! Arnold! (*Harry enters from* D. R. *Maude sees Harry.*) Darling! (*She stops dead. Her expression changes from anger to one of deep and yearning love. Harry is equally moved. There is a long silence as Harry comes to her. He raises his hands towards her and she takes them. Their faces come together and they go into a passionate embrace. After a couple of seconds Arnold's and Gilbert's heads come round the corner of the curtains [inner edge]. They stare in blank astonishment and then their heads go back behind the curtains. Harry and Maude break the embrace and gaze at each other.*) I thought we'd never meet again.

HARRY. It was only the night before last but it seems a million years ago.

MAUDE. And we never even knew each other's names.

HARRY. We knew enough, passion flower. (*Arnold's and Gilbert's heads come round again, outer edge.*) —The moon over the Mediterranean. (*Gilbert's and Arnold's heads disappear.*)

MAUDE. And the sand between our toes, smooth as silk.

HARRY. You won't get away from me this time.

MAUDE. (*Nods slowly.*) Mmm. (*They go off together through door* U. L., *leaving it open. Arnold emerges. He chuckles and does a little jump down the steps.*)

ARNOLD. (*To audience.*) This is a game for any number of players. (*Arnold opens Gilbert's curtain. Gilbert is crying like a baby.*)

GILBERT. (*Howling.*) My wife doesn't love me any more.

ARNOLD. Of course she does.

GILBERT. Then what the hell's she doing with 'orrible Harry?

ARNOLD. What you were hoping to do with 'orrible Harry's wife.

GILBERT. But Maude's doing it for nothing! Give me back my four-and-a-half thousand. (*Arnold gives it to Gilbert, who pockets it.*)

ARNOLD. There you are, Mr. Bodley. Aren't you going to give Janie the coat?

GILBERT. Am I, hell. (*Calls out.*) Janie! (*He opens the door* D. R.) You can come out now. (*Janie enters from storeroom* D. R., *leaving door open and stays by door.*)

JANIE. Everything all right?

76

GILBERT. Absolutely first class. (*Picks up Sue's dress from settee.*) Here's Mrs. Lawson's dress. Try that on for size and we'll tootle off together. (*He gives her Sue's dress.*)

JANIE. And you're going to give me everything you promised?

GILBERT. Definitely.

JANIE. And the mink and the car?

GILBERT. No, they're off but everything else is on.

JANIE. Oh, back where we started then. (*Janie gives Gilbert back the dress. She moves to the balcony, opens her coat and screams.*) Ahhh— (*Neither Gilbert nor Arnold has tried to stop her. She looks at them and her scream gets weaker. Gilbert sits C. of settee. Arnold sits chair R. of table.*)

GILBERT. Doesn't worry me. Does it worry you, Arnold?

ARNOLD. Not a bit. She can scream till she's blue in the—

GILBERT. Crouch!

JANIE. Well, what if Maude and Harry hear me?

ARNOLD. I can assure you they won't.

GILBERT. I'm sorry to have to tell you, but your husband and my wife are unfaithful.

JANIE. Both of them! With whom?

ARNOLD. Your wife and his husband.

JANIE. (*Astonished.*) I don't believe it.

GILBERT. It's true.

JANIE. (*Outraged.*) But we've been married for seven years— How can anyone behave like that!?

GILBERT. How indeed! But you'll get over it.

ARNOLD. Yes, it took you about ten seconds, didn't it?

JANIE. (*In a daze—taking Sue's dress from Gilbert and crossing him to storeroom D. R. and opening door.*) Well, I shall have to go home and lie down.

GILBERT. I'll join you as soon as I can.

JANIE. (*As she exits and closes door.*) Thank you. (*Arnold rises and crosses to Gilbert and sits L. of him on settee.*)

ARNOLD. Mr. Bodley, where had you thought of going to console each other?

GILBERT. Janie's flat.

ARNOLD. Maude and Harry might be there.

GILBERT. Might they? Well, my flat, then.

ARNOLD. Maude and Harry might be there.

GILBERT. Well, I'm too old for mixed doubles. (*Miss Tipdale enters from door* U. L., *leaves it open, wearing mink coat. She feels like a million dollars. She comes to top of steps* L. *Gilbert, rising and crossing towards her.*) Tippers!

ARNOLD. (*Rising.*) Miss Tipdale! What are you doing?

MISS TIPDALE. (*Crossing to between them.*) It's a present from Mrs. Bodley.

GILBERT. What for?

MISS TIPDALE. Hush money!

ARNOLD. Now that's poetic justice, and she didn't even have to be a good girl for it. (*The intercom phone rings. Gilbert picks it up, standing* R. *of table. Arnold and Miss Tipdale look at him.*)

GILBERT. (*Into phone.*) Hullo, Phillips— I thought you'd been fired. . . . (*Startled.*) You what? . . . I'll be right down. (*He slams the phone down and makes for the door* U. L.)

ARNOLD. What's the matter, Mr. Bodley?

GILBERT. I've got to go and see the doorman.

ARNOLD. Why?

GILBERT. He's going to sell his story to the Sunday papers! (*Gilbert exits door* U. L.)

ARNOLD. (*Turning to Miss Tipdale.*) You know, all this rushing around has had the most devastating effect on my adrenalin.

MISS TIPDALE. I'm delighted to hear it.

ARNOLD. Miss Tipdale?

MISS TIPDALE. Mr. Crouch?

ARNOLD. Ambrosine—?

MISS TIPDALE. Arnold—?

ARNOLD. Will you—? Will you—?

MRS. FRENCHAM. (*Entering from* U. L.) Will you tell my husband I've gone off home?

ARNOLD. Oh, yes. He was here a moment ago.

MRS. FRENCHAM. Oh!—missed him again! We shall never get our shopping done at this rate. (*Mr. Frencham gaily enters with 2 bottles of champagne.*)

MR. FRENCHAM. God, it's good to see you, Harriet.

MRS. FRENCHAM. George—where have you been? For goodness' sake, we've still got our shopping to do.

MR. FRENCHAM. Shopping, be damned! We're going back home immediately.

MRS. FRENCHAM. Home??

MR. FRENCHAM. Yes. Come on, my little peach. It's harvest

time! (*He smacks her bottom and they exit* U. L., *leaving door open.*)

ARNOLD. I think there must be something in the air.

MISS TIPDALE. You were saying, Mr. Crouch?

ARNOLD. Oh, yes. Miss Tipdale—Ambrosine—will you—will you— (*Sue comes out of cocktail cabinet* D. L., *carrying a champagne bottle. She is happily but mildly tipsy.*)

SUE. (*Brightly.*) Will you come help me, Mr. Crouch!? (*Sue shuts* D. L. *door. Miss Tipdale takes bottle and puts it on table.*)

MISS TIPDALE. Are you all right, Mrs. Lawson?

SUE. Lovely. (*To Arnold.*) Oh, Mr. Crouch, I think you're super. (*Putting arms round Arnold. Arnold reacts.*)

ARNOLD. I think you'd better go home now.

MISS TIPDALE. She can't—she only has bra and pants on under her coat.

ARNOLD. Oh no—she hasn't got a dress any more.

MISS TIPDALE. Well, she can have mine. (*Miss Tipdale takes off the mink.*)

SUE. Oh, that's a very pretty tip, Miss Dressdale.

MISS TIPDALE. Thank you very much. (*To Arnold.*) Mr. Crouch?

ARNOLD. Yes, Miss Tipdale? (*She turns her back to Arnold to be unzipped.*)

MISS TIPDALE. Undo me, will you? (*Arnold looks at audience and gives them a wicked wink.*)

ARNOLD. Yes, of course— Would you like to slip your coat off, Mrs. Lawson? (*Sue takes her coat off and Miss Tipdale slips out of her dress. Miss Tipdale is wearing a bright red slip. Arnold is overjoyed.*) My favorite color! (*Miss Tipdale and Arnold help Sue into the dress. While Miss Tipdale holds the dress open for Sue to step into it, Arnold gets on his knees to assist.*)

SUE. (*Stepping in, one foot at a time.*) One—two— (*They get the dress gathered up round her waist. Sue is facing Miss Tipdale with dress-zip at back. During Sue's next speech she turns first to Arnold and then to Miss Tipdale. Because they are holding the dress Sue turns, but the dress stays still. Sue, turning to Arnold.*) I think you're the nicest man I've ever met. (*Arnold looks up and finds her bosom level with his face. Sue, turning to Miss Tipdale.*) Don't you think he's nice, Miss Tipdale? (*As she turns, Arnold is now confronted with her bottom.*)

79

MISS TIPDALE. Yes, he is, very nice.

SUE. (*Turning to face Arnold again.*) You know the way you take the blame for everything is jelly gonerous. (*Arnold is riveted by the sight of her navel and quickly pulls the zip up but it gets stuck under her bosom. He tries to get it past, but to no avail.*)

ARNOLD. (*To audience.*) Anybody got a warm shoe horn? (*He goes back to dealing with her bosom.*)

GILBERT. (*Entering and seeing the situation.*) My God, he's a fast worker! (*Arnold gives up trying to get the zip past Sue's bosom, and neatly ties the two sleeves over her chest and grins at Gilbert.*)

ARNOLD. Ambrosine, it was on the tip of my tongue to propose to you just now.

MISS TIPDALE. Mr. Crouch, in answer to your request, I would be most happy to accept.

ARNOLD. Ambrosine.

MISS TIPDALE. Yes!

ARNOLD. May I kiss you?

MISS TIPDALE. Oh, yes. (*Arnold kisses Sue in mistake for Miss Tipdale. Lawson enters* U. L. *and sees this.*)

LAWSON. What the hell do you think you're doing?

GILBERT. It's all right, he's taking an inventory!

ARNOLD. I'm terribly sorry, just a little slip.

SUE. (*Zipping her dress up the front, and crossing to Lawson.*) Charlie, how dare you follow me here!

LAWSON. (*Grabbing her.*) You come with me. If this is how you carry on when my back's turned, we're going straight round to one of them legal fellows.

ARNOLD. Please, please. We've come through so much today, without resorting to divorce.

LAWSON. Who's talking about divorce? I'm going to marry her proper.

SUE. (*As she is pulled up steps by Lawson.*) Oh, Charlie! (*She turns in the doorway* U. L.) I'm going to be legitimate! (*They both exit* U. L., *Lawson pulling Sue after him. Janie enters door* D. R., *wearing Sue's dress. It is far too short and tight for her.*)

JANIE. Is it a bit short?

ARNOLD. Hardly worth putting on, was it?

MISS TIPDALE. Well, come to my office, and we'll see what we can do about it. (*Going up steps* C. *and towards door* U. L.)

JANIE. (Following her.) What do you suggest?

ARNOLD. I'll see if there's something I can let down!

MISS TIPDALE. Arnold! (Miss Tipdale exits U. L.)

GILBERT. (To Janie.) Hurry up, it's two o'clock and I'm hungry.

JANIE. (At door U. L.) Two minutes, darling. Then come back to my place and I'll give you a bite of something. (Janie exits U. L. as Gilbert reacts to her last remark.)

ARNOLD. Will you be safe?

GILBERT. I hope not! (Miss Whittington enters U. L.)

MISS WHITTINGTON. Do you want me for anything else, Mr. Bodley?

ARNOLD. Just tidy up in the storeroom, will you, Miss Whittington.

MISS WHITTINGTON. Certainly, Mr. Crouch. (She crosses seductively to D. R. and exits into storeroom, closing door behind her. Gilbert follows her to settee.)

GILBERT. (Looking towards door D. R.) How long did Janie say she'd be?

ARNOLD. Two minutes.

GILBERT. (Reflectively.) Two minutes— (Looks towards door R.—shakes his head and gives up the idea.) Come on, Arnold, let's go. (Gilbert exits U. L., followed by Arnold who re-enters immediately and runs towards D. R. eagerly, Gilbert re-enters before he reaches it, and stands watching him till he gets there.) Crouch! (Arnold starts violently, then rattles door handle.)

ARNOLD. It's locked! Definitely locked. Just checking. Make a note of that! (Arnold hurries back to Gilbert as:)

THE CURTAIN FALLS

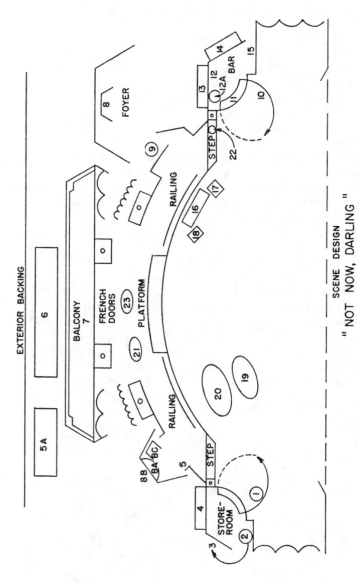

SCENE DESIGN
" NOT NOW, DARLING "
(Numbers shown correspond with those listed in Property Plot.)

EXTERIOR BACKING

FOYER

BALCONY
7

FRENCH
DOORS

PLATFORM

RAILING

RAILING

STEP

STEP

STORE-
ROOM

BAR

PROPERTY PLOT

Floor Covering: pale apricot color carpet

1. Storeroom door—mirrored front
   (closed)

2. Hooks for costumes—on back of return
   Mirror hanging on back of return
   Curtain to mask quick change room
   Ash tray for Bodley's cigar

3. Cabinets—*in*:
   Top—hangers
   2nd—papers, plastic covers
   3rd—box
   4th—furs

4. Cabinets—Below—2 boxes
   Bottom shelf—hat boxes, papers, proofs
   2nd shelf—proofs, 1 box
   3rd shelf—hangers
   4th shelf—(Top)—nothing—hang furs from shelves (on floor—
   boxes)

5. Standing ash tray

6. Stretcher to catch clothing, etc., and bamboo pole

7. French doors—closed

8. Chair—in hall

8A. Console table—fur magazines, glass vase with flowers

8B. Mirror—on wall

8C. Chair

9. Double doors
   n.—open—keyhole in door
   u.—closed

10. Bar door—closed

11. Refrigerator—*in*:
    Top shelf—ice trays
    Bottom shelf—Schweppes bottles
    Bottom shelf—3 bottles—leave space in center
    2nd shelf—8 highball glasses—Creme de cacao bottle
    3rd shelf—decanter and 8 martini stem glasses
    4th shelf—5 martini stem glasses
    Top shelf—3 decanters

12. 2 tea towels in catches

12A. Stool

13. Bottom shelf—(10) tall liquor bottles, ash tray
    2nd shelf—(7) tall liqueur bottles, champagne bucket
    Top shelf—7 bottles

14. Sink—
    2nd shelf—ice bucket and tongs, 3 highball glasses, 8 bottles
    3rd shelf—9 bottles

15. Shelf on back of return
    Mirror on back of return

16. Desk—secured to stage floor or railing
    French desk phone with dial—D. L. (phone wires tucked in railing)
    White interoffice phone—C.—(glued to table)
    Silver cigarette box with cigarettes in
    Cigarette lighter—on R. end of desk
    2 silver ash trays—1 is R. and D. corner—water in
    Matches
    L. drawer—diary

17. Chair

18. Chair—on—blue jacket with hankie (Crouch)

19. Oval fur rug

20. Oval settee—on—magazines

21. Dummy with legs (no arms or head)—on—beaver fur coat

22. Umbrella stand

23. Stool—mink brush

Off D. R. *Prop Table* (Storeroom)
Double of Sue's dress that Janie wears
Ocelot coat
Blazer (Crouch)

Off U.:
Mattress with rope
4 chairs
Mink coat with bra in pocket

Off U. L. (*Hall*) *Prop Table:*
Fur catalog, photostat proofs in clip folder, (Tipdale)
  Photos, proof pages in cellophane covers, clip
2 bottles of champagne (Bodley)
Umbrella with brown cover (Bodley)
Envelope with money in it (Bodley)
  in £1000 wads and all together
6 wads of 60 £ notes in wads of 10 (Harry)
Large boutique bag with bra and panties inside (Tipdale)
Shopping bag (Mrs. Frencham)
Overnight case (Maude)
2 full length beaver coats (Wardrobe) (Tipdale)
Double of Sue's dress (Harry)
2 bottles of champagne (Mr. Frencham)
Steno notebook (Tipdale)
Stud box (Maude)
Cigar (1 per performance) (Bodley)
Hat (Bodley)
Megaphone (Maude and Harry)

Off D. L. *Prop Table*—(Bar)
1. Tray—(Crouch)
   3 champagne glasses with champagne in

2. Champagne glass with champagne in (Crouch)
   2 dustbins,
   Broken glass, for glass crash
   Metal and tin lids

3. 2 glasses of champagne (Bodley)

4. 1 glass of champagne (Bodley)
   Champagne glass

5. 2 champagne glasses with champagne in (Crouch)
   (1 is ½ filled glass)
   Scotch bottle with tea in—top on (Sue)
   Empty champagne bottle (Sue)

85

6. Set on tray:
    2 champagne glasses with champagne in (Crouch)
    (Both 1/3 filled)
    Open bottle of champagne—with champagne in
    4 full, unopened champagne bottles
    1 empty champagne bottle
    1 ½ filled champagne bottle
    11 glasses (champagne)

PERSONAL PROPS

Lady's wristwatch (Tipdale)

Man's wristwatch (Harry)

Keys on key ring (Maude)

Gold pencil on neck chain (Tipdale)

Man's wristwatch (Crouch)

Glasses (Tipdale)

Man's wristwatch (Bodley)

Handkerchief (Crouch)

COSTUME LIST

MAUDE BODLEY:
Aqua 2 piece suit
White hat
White bag
White gloves
2 pair pantihose
White shoes
2 rings
Earrings
Purple dress
Black handbag
Black shoes
Earrings
8 fine chains
2 rings

JANIE McMICHAEL
Pink trick dress
2 Pucci bras—fitted and covered
2 pair Pucci pants
2 pair nude briefs
2 prop bras and 2 prop pants
2 pair pantihose
Garter belt
Bra with tea towel tricked on
Tea towel skirt
2 pair bust pads
4 pair stockings
4 pair grey stockings
Grey bag
Grey shoes
4 rings
Earrings
Lime polka dot dress (Sue double)
Green crepe dress (Sue double)
Green tricot print dress (Sue double)
Beaver coat
Silver mink coat

ARNOLD CROUCH:
All his own clothes, except:
White furrier's coat
4 white shirts

GILBERT BODLEY:
All his own clothes

HARRY McMICHAEL:
Suit
3 pair sox
Suspenders
Cuff links
2 white shirts
Tie

MR. LAWSON:
Slacks and sport jacket
4 knit shirts
3 pair sox
Shoes

MR. FRENCHAM:
Brown blazer
Brown slacks
2 shirts
3 ties
Blazer emblem
Brown suspenders
3 pair sox
Cuff links
Brown shoes

SUE LAWSON:
Green polka dot dress
Green print tricot dress
Green crepe dress
2 pink padded bras
2 pair pink panties
2 pair pantihose
Hand bag
Shoes
Beaver coat
Blue beads
Rings

MISS TIPDALE:
  Rust dress
  Beige dress
  Aqua dress
  2 red bras
  2 pair red panties
  2 pair pantihose
  Shoes

MISS WHITTINGTON:
  Grey dress
  2 pair pantihose
  Pink beads
  Padded bra

MRS. FRENCHAM:
  White print dress
  White hat
  Handbag
  White gloves
  Shoes
  Earrings
  Fur coat

NEW PLAYS

★ **AS BEES IN HONEY DROWN by Douglas Carter Beane.** Winner of the John Gassner Playwriting Award. A hot young novelist finds the subject of his new screenplay in a New York socialite who leads him into the world of *Auntie Mame* and *Breakfast at Tiffany's*, before she takes him for a ride. "A delicious soufflé of a satire … [an] extremely entertaining fable for an age that always chooses image over substance." –*The NY Times* "… A witty assessment of one of the most active and relentless industries in a consumer society … the creation of 'hot' young things, which the media have learned to mass produce with efficiency and zeal." –*The NY Daily News* [3M, 3W, flexible casting] ISBN: 0-8222-1651-5

★ **STUPID KIDS by John C. Russell.** In rapid, highly stylized scenes, the story follows four high-school students as they make their way from first through eighth period and beyond, struggling with the fears, frustrations, and longings peculiar to youth. "In STUPID KIDS … playwright John C. Russell gets the opera of adolescence to a T … The stylized teenspeak of STUPID KIDS … suggests that Mr. Russell may have hidden a tape recorder under a desk in study hall somewhere and then scoured the tapes for good quotations … it is the kids' insular, ceaselessly churning world, a pre-adult world of Doritos and libidos, that the playwright seeks to lay bare." –*The NY Times* "STUPID KIDS [is] a sharp-edged … whoosh of teen angst and conformity anguish. It is also very funny." –*NY Newsday* [2M, 2W] ISBN: 0-8222-1698-1

★ **COLLECTED STORIES by Donald Margulies.** From Obie Award-winner Donald Margulies comes a provocative analysis of a student-teacher relationship that turns sour when the protégé becomes a rival. "With his fine ear for detail, Margulies creates an authentic, insular world, and he gives equal weight to the opposing viewpoints of two formidable characters." –*The LA Times* "This is probably Margulies' best play to date …" –*The NY Post* "… always fluid and lively, the play is thick with ideas, like a stock-pot of good stew." –*The Village Voice* [2W] ISBN: 0-8222-1640-X

★ **FREEDOMLAND by Amy Freed.** An overdue showdown between a son and his father sets off fireworks that illuminate the neurosis, rage and anxiety of one family – and of America at the turn of the millennium. "FREEDOMLAND's more obvious links are to *Buried Child* and *Bosoms and Neglect*. Freed, like Guare, is an inspired wordsmith with a gift for surreal touches in situations grounded in familiar and real territory." –*Curtain Up* [3M, 4W] ISBN: 0-8222-1719-8

★ **STOP KISS by Diana Son.** A poignant and funny play about the ways, both sudden and slow, that lives can change irrevocably. "There's so much that is vital and exciting about STOP KISS … you want to embrace this young author and cheer her onto other works … the writing on display here is funny and credible … you also will be charmed by its heartfelt characters and up-to-the-minute humor." –*The NY Daily News* "… irresistibly exciting … a sweet, sad, and enchantingly sincere play." –*The NY Times* [3M, 3W] ISBN: 0-8222-1731-7

★ **THREE DAYS OF RAIN by Richard Greenberg.** The sins of fathers and mothers make for a bittersweet elegy in this poignant and revealing drama. "… a work so perfectly judged it heralds the arrival of a major playwright … Greenberg is extraordinary." –*The NY Daily News* "Greenberg's play is filled with graceful passages that are by turns melancholy, harrowing, and often, quite funny." –*Variety* [2M, 1W] ISBN: 0-8222-1676-0

★ **THE WEIR by Conor McPherson.** In a bar in rural Ireland, the local men swap spooky stories in an attempt to impress a young woman from Dublin who recently moved into a nearby "haunted" house. However, the tables are soon turned when she spins a yarn of her own. "You shed all sense of time at this beautiful and devious new play." –*The NY Times* "Sheer theatrical magic. I have rarely been so convinced that I have just seen a modern classic. Tremendous." –*The London Daily Telegraph* [4M, 1W] ISBN: 0-8222-1706-6

DRAMATISTS PLAY SERVICE, INC.
440 Park Avenue South, New York, NY 10016 212-683-8960 Fax 212-213-1539
postmaster@dramatists.com   www.dramatists.com